Bedfordshire RE Series

WORLD RELIGIONS

Compiled by

Graham McFarlane
& Barry Pinder

Editorial Group

Cath Large – Head of RE, Putteridge High School, Luton
Martin Rowland-Thomas – Head of Humanities,
Holmemead Middle School, Biggleswade
Graham McFarlane – Head of Multiracial Education Resources
Centre, Luton
Richard Hancock – County Inspector for English and Drama
Mark Gamble – Schools Development Officer, TMRS

Series Editor: Rachel Gregory

Teaching Media Resource Service

Published and distributed by
**TMRS, Russell House, 14 Dunstable Street, Ampthill, Beds. MK45 2JT for
Bedfordshire Education Service,
Chief Education Officer: D. P. J. Browning, CBE, M.A.**

© **Copyright Bedfordshire Education Service 1986**

First published April 1986

ISBN 0 907 041 49 3 4

Photoset by Millford Reprographics International Ltd., Luton, Beds.
Printed by Kenley Press Ltd., Dunstable, Beds.

Cover photograph by Ken Whitbread

CONTENTS

INTRODUCTION

This booklet on 'World Religions' attempts to provide some basic background information on world religions whilst recognising the diversity that exists within every faith. The booklet is mainly concerned with six major world religions, but there are also short sections on two of the many other religious groups that are present in multi-faith Bedfordshire. The booklet is written with the needs of the non-specialist RE teacher in mind. A good selection of reference books on 'World Religions' is essential for the more detailed information needed for curriculum development purposes, and at the end of each section are suggestions for further reading. Schools developing curriculum initiatives concerning world religions are also encouraged to involve members of the local faith communities.

The Bedfordshire Agreed Syllabus for Religious Education complements national and local policy statements on education in, and for, a multi-ethnic society. The H.M. Government report 'Education for All' and the Bedfordshire county policy statement 'Policies for a Multi-cultural Community' provide clear evidence for and commitment towards a multicultural, anti-racist approach to curriculum development in all schools. A study of world religions and the use of thematic approaches which include references to world religions are an excellent focus for that multi-cultural, anti-racist initiative, vitally important to the future of our community.

CHRONOLOGICAL CHART

2500 BCE	2000 BCE	1500 BCE	1000 BCE	500 BCE
HINDUISM				
	JUDAISM			
				BUDDHI...

Where dates are given, the modern practice of using BCE (Before Common Era) and CE (Common Era) has been adopted. These correspond to BC and AD.

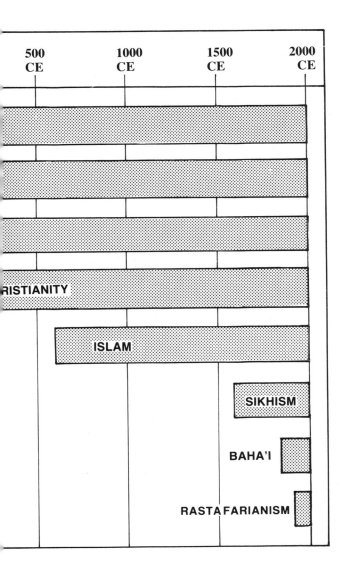

500 CE	1000 CE	1500 CE	2000 CE

CHRISTIANITY

ISLAM

SIKHISM

BAHA'I

RASTAFARIANISM

3

HINDUISM

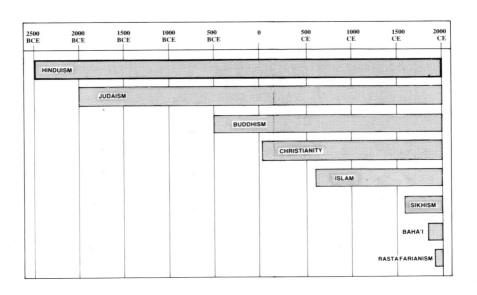

2500 BCE	2000 BCE	1500 BCE	1000 BCE	500 BCE	0	500 CE	1000 CE	1500 CE	2000 CE
HINDUISM									
	JUDAISM								
			BUDDHISM						
				CHRISTIANITY					
					ISLAM				
								SIKHISM	
								BAHA'I	
								RASTAFARIANISM	

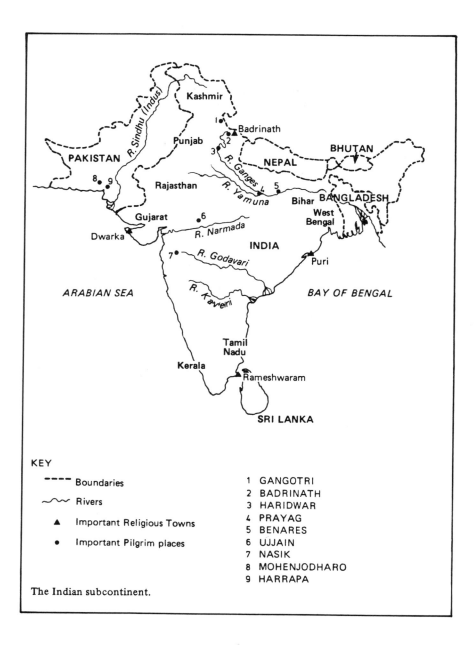

KEY

- - - - Boundaries

~~~~ Rivers

▲ Important Religious Towns

• Important Pilgrim places

1 GANGOTRI
2 BADRINATH
3 HARIDWAR
4 PRAYAG
5 BENARES
6 UJJAIN
7 NASIK
8 MOHENJODHARO
9 HARRAPA

The Indian subcontinent.

HINDUISM

ORIGINS

Aspects of Hinduism make it mankind's oldest living religious tradition. The names Hinduism, Hindu and India are derived from the Sanskrit word Sindhu, an ancient name for the River Indus in North-West India. The term Hindu was in time applied to those who inhabited the land beyond the Sindhu, and Hinduism eventually became a composite description for the multitude of religious ideas expressed by the peoples of this vast area, the Indian sub-continent.

The earliest known civilisation of the Indian sub-continent flourished around the Indus valley some two thousand years before the common era and its religion possessed several features which appear in later Hinduism. This urban civilisation possibly began to decay around 1750 BCE* at the time of migrations from Central Asia by peoples termed Aryan. They brought the idea of the *caste* system which remains an important aspect of Hindu culture. The great diversity of beliefs and practices within Hinduism may be accounted for by the merging of these two very different civilisations.

Most of the people of India are Hindus, forming 80% of its population and there have always been Hindus in countries bordering India such as Nepal, Sri Lanka, Pakistan and Bangladesh. Migration spread the religion to South-East Asia and more recently to South and East Africa, Britain, Canada, the United States and Australia. Offshoots of Hinduism have become popular sects within some of these countries e.g. the Hare Krishna Movement and Mahesh Yogi Transcendental Meditation Centres. The religions of Buddhism and Sikhism share common roots with Hinduism.

BASIC BELIEFS

It is not appropriate to talk of Hindu dogma as it is behaviour that matters to the Hindu. Since Hinduism developed gradually over many centuries and has no founder, its main beliefs and religious ideas are varied and not always accepted by all schools of thought within Hinduism. However, there are some fundamental concepts that the vast majority of adherents would acknowledge as important elements.

---

* Where dates are given the modern practice of using BCE (Before Common Era) and CE (Common Era) has been adopted. These correspond to BC and AD.

God

To non-Hindus it may appear that Hindus are polytheistic because they recognise thousands of images of God – some in the form of human beings, others in animal or abstract form. However, Hindus claim that each image and indeed all things within the Universe are aspects of the one God, *Brahman* or *Paramatma*.

Brahman is eternal, omnipotent and the sole Reality. Brahman is within all things and is all things. Everything is an expression of Brahman and, though in essence formless, Brahman may be manifest in any form for the fulfilment of a purpose.

Three manifestations of Brahman are particularly significant within Hinduism: *Brahma*, the Creator, *Vishnu*, the Preserver and *Shiva*, the Destroyer. Collectively these gods relate to the Hindu idea that it is Brahman who creates, sustains and destroys the Universe within a sequence of cycles, within which there are a series of ages, each marking a progressive decline in the virtue, longevity and contentment of humankind. Brahma, Vishnu and Shiva are sometimes called the *Trimurti* or the Hindu Trinity.

Many Hindus believe in *avatars* (incarnations) of Brahman. In particular the god Vishnu is said to have ten avatars, one yet to come. In practice only two are widely recognised in worship: *Krishna*, the hero of the Sanskrit epic, the *Mahabharata*, and *Rama*, the hero of the other popular scripture, the *Ramayana* (see 'Important Books'). In all, the Hindu scriptures contain many names for Brahman and many visual and abstract symbols are used. One such symbol is *OM*, pronounced 'aum', a sound-image of Brahman. It occurs in many verses within Hindu writings and is often sounded during worship.

8

Atma

Part of Brahman is in all things. This is called the *atma* and it is sometimes designated the spiritual self or soul. Hindus view the atma as unborn, unchangeable and indestructible. The goal of existence is to facilitate the merger of the atma with Brahman which is only attainable when an individual becomes totally conscious of the atma within himself and this is rarely achieved within a single lifetime.

Samsara

This is the concept of the cycle of re-birth (re-incarnation). Another aspect of the soul is termed the *jeevatma* which is influenced and altered by the experience of living. When Hindus speak of re-incarnation it is the jeevatma of an individual being reborn into another existence determined by its own state which is the cumulative effect of past experience. The cycle of births and deaths persists until the atma merges with Brahman. Once this level of awareness has been achieved that aspect of the soul termed the jeevatma ceases to function since the soul is liberated from worldly experience. This state of liberation is called *Moksha* or *Mukti*. The methods of attaining Moksha and the relationship between the atma and jeevatma are described in the Hindu Scriptures often in allegorical form.

Karma

Connected with re-incarnation is the doctrine of *karma*; that every action has its reaction. This law leads the soul from one existence to the next until it has purified itself through meritorious action and unites with Brahman. The notion of karma is also linked with two further important concepts within Hinduism: *caste* and *dharma*.

Caste

The Hindu Scriptures forward the philosophy that individuals differ in their capabilities and inclinations and this results from spiritual forces beyond human control. Hindu society has, therefore, been divided into four *varnas* or *castes* and a person's position within the system is believed to be determined by previous existences. This gives the system its spiritual dimension. Though Hindu Scriptures promote the idea that each caste is of equal value to the society and should be accorded parity of status, they do not advocate equal opportunities, associating this extent of inequality with the varying effects of karma.

In practice over the centuries divisions in the society have assumed the form of high and low, though the current Indian constitution makes it illegal to refer to a person as low-caste. Efforts are being made to produce conditions that will enable all to enjoy the facilities of education, social development and civil rights.

The four main varnas, which refers to 'estates' rather than caste, though the two are often regarded as synonymous, are:

Brahmins – those whose contribution to society is centred on intellectual, priestly and advisory tasks;

Kshatriyas – those responsible for maintaining law, protecting the people through good government and giving military service;

Vaishyas – those more inclined to roles within trade, commerce, industrial and agricultural production;

Shudras – those concerned with manual labour rather than intellectual service

Within this broad framework there exist many castes and sub-castes, each following a specific occupation.

Mahatma Gandhi, perhaps the foremost figure within modern Indian nationalism, did not oppose the caste system suggesting that it was mirrored in all societies. However, he vehemently opposed the attitude that the lowest of the Shudras, those whose jobs were the dirtiest and therefore brought ritual impurity upon them, should be deemed untouchable. He renamed the Untouchables *Harijan*, which means 'children of God' and led a campaign to end what he saw as the inhuman treatment given to this vast number of fellow human beings.

The scriptural foundation of the caste system and therefore its divine nature, has led to rigidity within it. Each caste is normally endogamous (marriage occurring within the group) and relations with other castes are distant. One scripture, the Bhagavad Gita, says 'It is better to risk even death in the performance of one's own duties (related to caste) than to attempt to perform what is assigned to others'. This concept of duty is termed *Dharma*.

Dharma

Dharma is a Sanskrit word which refers to the essential nature of all things. As the dharma of fire is to burn so the ancient scriptures, the Vedas, teach that the dharma of all beings is to serve others. People must follow the dharma inherent with their particular position. Beyond the dharma of a person's physical situation which is impermanent, there is the eternal dharma of the atma (soul), which is to render service to Brahman (God) with devotion. For some Hindus, the world we see is not real but *maya* (illusion) which causes them to lose their awareness of their duty. Through following one of the Hindu paths of liberation Hindus can break through *maya* and achieve *moksha*.

Within this framework of beliefs there is the overall goal of *Moksha* – release from the bonds of transmigration. Unlike those religious traditions where dogma is possibly more pre-eminent, Hinduism accepts a number of quite different viable paths (*margas*) to *Moksha*. There is *karma-marga*, the way of unselfish action motivated by duty rather than by personal gain; *Bhakti-marga* the way of loving devotion whereby God's grace is given; and *jnana-marga*, the way of inner knowledge often involving the practice of yoga.

IMPORTANT BOOKS

There are several holy scriptures in Hinduism, the most sacred being the *Vedas*, the oldest religious scriptures in use, and the *Upanishads*.

The Sanskrit word 'veda' means divine knowledge and the majority of the verses deal with how humankind should conduct itself in life, the performance of rituals and the consequences of actions. This knowledge is said to be revealed by God and contains universal and eternal truths. The texts were composed some time between 1500 BCE and 500 BCE and were initially transferred orally until being committed to written form much later.

The name Upanishad has its roots in three Sanskrit words meaning 'near-down-sit'. These scriptures contain the discourse between teachers (*gurus*) and students sitting down together. These discussions are presented in prose and verse and centre on the more philosophical facets of Hinduism. They date from around 500 BCE.

The *Vedas* has four divisions called *Rig*, *Yajur*, *Atharva* and *Sama*. The *Rig-Veda* is the oldest and most important. It consists of around one thousand hymns arranged in ten sections each containing a series of verses called *mantras*. Most of the hymns and prayers used in Hindu worship are taken from Vedic texts or the Upanishads.

Commentaries on the Vedic scriptures were made later and codes of regulations based upon Vedic principles were formulated.

In order to convey the basic eternal and spiritual truths of the Vedas, many further texts were written often in the form of mythological story. Two of these are the epics the *Mahabarata* and the *Ramayana*.

The Mahabarata contains 110,000 verses making it the longest poem in the world. It details the exploits of mythological heroes. A small section of it is called the *Bhagavad Gita* (the Song of the Lord). This has become a highly revered text because of its exposition of Vedic religious understanding. It recalls discussions between two characters, Arjuna and his charioteer Krishna (an avatar of the god Vishnu). The discussions reveal the nature of the relationship between Brahman and humankind as well as the means to salvation, and teach *Bhakti* – the devotional form of Hinduism most prevalent today.

The other epic poem is the *Ramayana* which consists of around 24,000 verses. The story contained within it is frequently related through drama and dance during festivals. The story focuses on the adventures of the great and just Prince Rama (another avatar of Vishnu) whose wife, Sita, is forcibly taken away to Sri Lanka by the demon Ravana and is later rescued following great battles. It is a classic good versus evil tale of immense ethical significance within Hinduism.

IMPORTANT BUILDINGS

Although Hindu homes usually contain a shrine, a place of personal worship, the Temple (*Mandir*) has special significance in the life of many people. Hindus think of the temple as a house for the deity which is worshipped there. Each temple may be dedicated to one or more of the Hindu gods.

The principal feature of any temple is the shrine room in which the image of the god is placed. Hindus believe that Brahman is present in the temple in the form of the image in order to render possible the devotees worship. Around the main shrine smaller ones honouring other deities of less importance to the worshippers may be located.

Above the shrine-room there may be a domed tower emphasising the honour due and symbolising a mountain which is considered sacred. In front of the shrine room there is a hall at the entrance to which is a porch facing the shrine. A courtyard often surrounds the main building and around the inside of this may be found a covered way for processions. There may also be a tank of water within the site since bathing is an important religious ritual.

Larger temples may contain halls used for temple dancing, schools and libraries for study of the scriptures, offices for managing the temple's business, sheds for processional chariots, gardens to grow flowers and food used in worship and living quarters for personnel.

Though the main function of a temple is as a place of worship, some have become community centres, places of public celebration at festival times and objects of pilgrimage.

IMPORTANT FESTIVALS

Throughout the Hindu year there are a large number of festivals and sacred holidays, each of which has its own unique character to be observed in a particular manner and mood. Some only take place within certain regional communities. More universally accepted ones may be celebrated in different ways in different Indian states and different stories or interpretations of traditional stories may lie at the heart of those festivities. So what follows can only claim to be a glimpse of Hindu religious festivals.

Within Hinduism festivals are integrated with a lunar calendar. They are mentioned here in cyclical order.

Rama-Navami is celebrated on the ninth day of the first month Chait'r. The occasion is Rama's birthday and extracts from the Ramayana outlining the key events in the hero's life feature in the worship offered. An image of Rama may be carried in procession.

Raksha Bandhan takes place during the months of Shraavan and its name originates from the practice of women tying coloured silk threads around the wrists of male relatives and friends. The tie establishes a platonic relationship within which the man is obligated to protect the honour of the woman and her family.

Janmashtami also falls in the month of Shraavan and is a celebration of the birth of Krishna, the hero of the Bhagavad Gita. Fasting takes place until midnight and then the nativity is celebrated with song and dance recalling Krishna's exploits. At home, devotees may display a crib, and special sweet foods are made similar to those consumed by nursing mothers.

Navaratri occurs at the beginning of Ashwin and is a nine-day festival devoted to the goddess *Durga*. Navaratri means 'nine nights' though the occasion is called *Durga Puja* in Northern India. Dramatic representation of the main incidents recorded in the Ramayana is an important feature, particularly the assistance given to Rama by Durga in the conflict with Ravana. In Bengal a special poem called the *Chandi* will be read recalling how Durga triumphed over evil and an image of Durga will be submerged in a river symbolising the ceasing of unhappiness and misfortune.

Dashera comes at the end of Navaratri and literally means 'the tenth'. It recalls the day of the defeat and death of Ravana and huge effigies of Ravana and other mythological demons will be filled with fireworks, carried in procession and finally set alight.

Diwali is probably the most popularly celebrated festival and is regarded as the New Year in some parts of India. It falls in the months of Ashwin and Kartik and lasts two to five days. Diwali is a shortened form of the word *Deepavali* which means a row of lamps (*devas*). These are simple oil (ghee) lamps that are placed inside and outside temples and homes. Some Hindus see the devas as lighting the path of *Lakshmi*, the goddess of prosperity whilst others recall the triumphal return of Rama and Sita to their kingdom following the defeat of Ravana as recorded in the Ramayana. The occasion is regarded as a time of renewal following the settling of debts and disputes. Presents and greetings cards are exchanged, friends and relatives visited and there are special foods and sweets.

Shivarati is the 'night consecrated to Shiva' and it takes place in the month of Maagh. It is a fairly solemn occasion marked by fasting and worship throughout the night by ardent devotees of this deity.

Holi is the final public festival within the Hindu calendar and takes place in the month of Phaalgun at the time of the Spring harvest season in India. It lasts between two and five days and is characterised by the lighting of bonfires and much carefree joy involving the splashing of coloured water and throwing red and violet powder dyes over people. An explanation of the former focuses on the story of a demon called *Holika* who attempted to burn *Prahlada*, a devout worshipper of Vishnu, but whose attempts only led to his own destruction. The latter actions centre on the blossoming love between *Krishna* and his favourite devotee, *Radha*, and the general romantic and mischievous nature of his personality. The stories are read and enacted within the home and temple.

IMPORTANT RELIGIOUS PRACTICES

Worship

This has three aspects:

1   Household ritual, often based on sixteen *Samskaras* (sacraments). Each has its own method and detail but a common feature is the offering of oblations to the sacred fire accompanied by the chanting of Sanskrit mantras.

2   Temple worship, which is often extended into the home since every home should have a shrine as the focal point of the family's religious life.

3   Meditation through yoga deemed to be the highest form of worship. The word yoga literally means the act of uniting, or yoking, together two things, that is, the individual soul (atma) and God (Brahman).

The most common form of worship performed in the home is called *Puja* and it is carried out before the image of a god often chosen because of family or community tradition. The image is kept within the shrine and before entering a person is expected to have bathed and put on clean clothes. Shoes are removed prior to entry and all of the items required for worship such as dishes, food, flowers and incense will have been gathered together.

Following these preparations the worshipper invites the spirit of God to attend the image through the ringing of a bell. The image, located on a raised platform, is ceremonially washed, decorated with garlands and anointed with perfumes. Flowers and specially prepared foods are offered whilst incense is burned before the image. Worship symbolically incorporates and binds the basic elements of existence.

The devotee then places his or her hands together and raises them to the forehead and offers prayers.

Worship takes place in the temple with a priest officiating and may include other features in addition to those mentioned:

Havan (Homa) – the kindling of a fire from prescribed woods and fragrant substances which is burnt before the image;

Aarti – a ghee lamp is waved before the image and passed around the congregation who symbolically receive God's blessing by passing their hands over the flame and then over their own forehead and hair;

Prasad – food offered to the image becomes blessed and is distributed;

Bhajans – hymns sung to the accompaniment of musical instruments and clapping.

All forms of worship are intended to foster a greater awareness of Brahman and the presence of Brahman in all things. Although not rigid in format many aspects of worship are prescribed in the Scriptures.

Pilgrimage

Within Hinduism pilgrimage is regarded as another act through which religious merit can be achieved. There are numerous shrines and temples considered by Hindus to be of religious significance and they are situated throughout India. Perhaps the most important are the Jagannath Temple at Puri, the Temple of Rameshwaram, on an island between the Indian mainland and Sri Lanka, and the Temples of Dwaraka on the coast of Gujarat, and at Badrinath in the Himalayas.

Hindus also view many of their rivers with reverence and respect. They represent the life-giving nature of Brahman, and bathing symbolises spiritual cleansing. The River Ganges is particularly important and centres of pilgrimage have developed at Hardwar where it descends from the sacred mountains and at Benares (Varanasi). After the Ganges in importance is the River Jumna (Yamuna) with important centres at Mathura and Vrindavan. Other rivers including the *Sindhu* (*Indus*), are also considered holy. All are associated with events in Hindu mythology, and, since river-side sites were important locations for study, they became centres of Hindu scholarship.

Food and Fasting

The preparation and presentation of foodstuffs (prasad) is a particularly important facet of worship. There are twenty-eight feasts, fasts and festivals within the Hindu calendar and special symbolic foods are prepared on some occasions, whilst on others only specified foods may be eaten or abstained from. Fasting is done in honour of a deity and religious merit is acquired.

Vegetarianism is important within Hindu culture and this is related to the core belief that the atma, the life-force or soul, is present in all living things and therefore to sacrifice animal food is inappropriate behaviour. However, the veneration of the cow has as much to do with its practical usefulness as to tradition based on Scriptures.

Rites of Passage

For a person born into the religion, Hinduism provides a framework that gives an overall purpose to human life. It offers guidance on every identifiable stage in the physical and spiritual development of people.

The Hindu Scriptures divide an individual's life-cycle into four periods known as *ashramas* or stages which, like the caste system, form an important aspect of the Hindu social and spiritual system, though in a model rather than rigidly enforceable sense. Each ashrama is punctuated with specific rites or sacraments called *samskaras* and there are sixteen of these. Samskaras means 'preparatory process'.

The first stage or ashrama is a period of general education, professional training, preparation for family life, citizenship and religious responsibility. The second, is a period as householder and active worker. The third stage is a period of retirement in preparation for stage four which is a time of total renunciation of the world when all family and community ties are severed.

There are eleven samskaras corresponding to the first ashrama and these centre on the upbringing of a child. Two are particularly important:

The Naming Ceremony (Naamadheya)

This takes place eleven or twelve days after the birth. The name must be auspicious, perhaps that of a deity or mythological hero e.g. Rama,

Krishna or Sita. The name may reflect the qualities that the parents wish their child to possess or be an expression of the belief that God has blessed them with a child e.g. Lalita ('charming') or Devadatta ('given by the god').

The Sacred Thread Ceremony (Upanayana)

This rite occurs between the eighth and twelfth birthdays of a boy dependent upon his caste though Shudras are not initiated. The boy is invested with a sacred white thread, composed of three strands representing the Hindu Trinity, so that it rests on the left shoulder and hangs across the boy's chest down to his right thigh. The boy has become *dvija* ('twice-born') and the sacrament qualifies him to commence his study of the Vedic scriptures.

Two further samskaras are highly significant:

Marriage (Vivaaha)

Marriage is the most important sacrament within the second ashrama. Parents attempt to ensure that the couple are from comparable caste backgrounds and that their horoscopes are a good match. Marriage is an alliance of two families and following the initial investigations the betrothal is announced and the wedding day set.

The marriage day begins with a ceremony through which the father formally gives his daughter in marriage. The wedding itself takes place around the sacred fire (*homa*) and perhaps the most significant ritual is when the husband leads his wife in the seven steps around the fire whilst symbolically secured to her with a piece of material. Vows are made and sacred mantras spoken.

The final samskara deals with funeral rites:

Funeral (Antyeshti)

The Scriptures prescribe the procedure for cremation, the items to be used in the burning, the oblations to be offered and the mantras to be spoken. If it is possible the funeral pyre will be built near a sacred river though in urban centres a modern crematorium will be used. The ashes will be scattered into the flowing river sometimes from steps called *ghats*.

The central belief is that after cremation the body has once again become part of the basic elements of existence and the atma (soul) awaits the time when it enters another form.

HINDUISM

For further reading:

Brockington, J. L.	THE SACRED THREAD	Univ. of Edinburgh Press
Hopkins, T.	THE HINDU RELIGIOUS TRADITION	Wadsworth
Killingley, D. (ed)	A HANDBOOK OF HINDUISM FOR TEACHERS	Grevatt & Grevatt
Kinsley, D. R.	HINDUISM	Prentice Hall
Koller, J. M.	THE INDIAN WAY	Macmillan, N.Y.
Stutley, M.	HINDUISM, THE ETERNAL LAW	Aquarian Press

JUDAISM

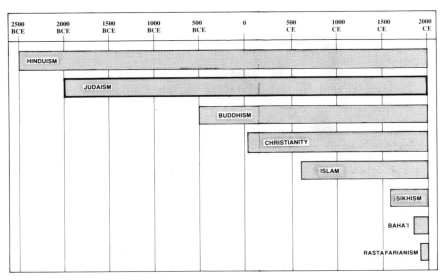

JUDAISM

ORIGINS

Judaism began about 4,000 years ago in the area known as the Middle East. The beginnings of the Jewish faith can be identified with the *Patriarchs*, the 'Fathers' of the religion. The 'Fathers' were Abraham, Isaac and Jacob, with Abraham as the single most important figure in the origins of Judaism. It was Abraham who developed the concept of One God, and the *covenant* between God and the Hebrews (the tribe of Abraham), who later were to be called the Israelites.

BASIC BELIEFS

The basic beliefs can be summed up in five main areas:

1 Belief in the Existence of a Creator

God – there is only one God, the creator of the Universe, to whom all prayers are addressed. He is considered to be above all creatures and hears all their prayers.

2 Belief in the Words of the Prophets

Prophets – it is a basic belief within Judaism that Moses was the greatest of all prophets and that the *Torah* was revealed to Moses at Sinai.

3 Belief in the Unchangeable Nature of the Revealed Law

Although certain practices differ between Orthodox and Liberal/Reform Jews, the basic belief in the revealed Law is central. This includes the belief in the concept of a '*Chosen People*'. Jews believe a special relationship exists between God and Jewish people. God gave the Jews his Law so they regard themselves as having been chosen by Him. The importance of this lies in the undertaking of special duties and obligations. Charity, for example, plays a large part in the Jewish way of life and is seen as a basic Jewish duty. To this can be linked a feeling of community which ensures that the aged and infirm are cared for.

Jews are said to carry God's message to the world but at the same time Judaism is not a proselytising or missionary faith. Other faiths have a place in God's order so long as people live their lives with love, respect and care for others.

4 Belief in Retribution in this World and in the Hereafter

Good and Evil – since God is good, people therefore should be good. This implies that Jews should love everyone as well as God. If people do evil things they can have God's forgiveness if they repent. A basic Jewish belief is in the resurrection of the dead. Jews believe that God, as well as judge, is also merciful.

5 Belief in the Coming of the Messiah

Jews believe in the coming of a Messiah who will bring peace and harmony into the world. Jews still await the coming of the Messianic age.

IMPORTANT PEOPLE

Abraham – Abraham lived about 2000 BCE. His nomadic existence centred around Ur in the Middle East, but he travelled widely in many countries. He finally settled in Canaan, later called Palestine, where Jewish scripture describes him as being called by God. This calling resulted in the 'covenant' between Abraham and God. This covenant was renewed with Isaac, Abraham's son, and Jacob, his grandson. When Jacob renewed the promises of the covenant i.e. to serve God and worship Him only, he was, according to Genesis 32 v.28, divinely given the additional name '*Israel*'. His descendants became known as the '*children of Israel*'.

Moses – Moses was born in Egypt to Israelite parents in about 1300 BCE. Moses' story is told in the Book of Exodus. Moses became a leader of the Israelites and eventually led this people out of Egyptian slavery into freedom. Moses led the Israelites through the desert to the foot of Mount Sinai, where Moses climbed the mountain to renew the covenant with God. This covenant was now between God and His people, the Israelites. It meant the people accepted God's Law, the basis of which was the Ten Commandments. In return the people believed that God had specially chosen them to be His people and that through them the world would come to know God and learn to live in peace and unity.

Moses played an essential part in the establishment of the Jewish faith, and the Jews believe him to be the greatest prophet. The first five books of the Bible are known as the '*Books of Moses*' and form the Torah.

Since Patriarchal times there have been a succession of respected Jewish scholars who have shaped the religion through the centuries.

IMPORTANT BOOKS

The first five books of Moses are the most important to Jews and contain the origins of Judaism and the basic laws. These are the sacred books which form the scrolls which are read regularly in the synagogue. They are called the *Torah*, and are seen as the revealed word of God, the basis of the religion and source of its faith. Use is made of the rest of the Old Testament especially the Prophets and Psalms.

There are two further important books, which are revered. These are the *Talmud*, which is a discussion of the Bible covering every subject of life concerning Judaism; and the *Mishnah*, which further interprets and explains Jewish laws and stories from the Bible.

All the above books, especially the Torah, are very important in that they have a central place both in public worship in the synagogue and in private prayer. The reading of the Torah is the most important part of the service in the synagogue on the Sabbath.

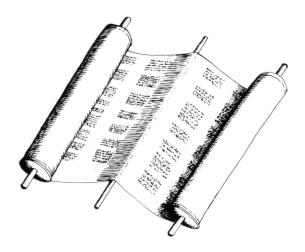

IMPORTANT BUILDINGS

The Synagogue – Prayer can take place anywhere but the main religious building is the Synagogue (or, in Hebrew, the *Shul*). This is the Jewish meeting place and house of prayer and its concept dates back over two thousand years. The synagogue may also be the community centre containing classroom and offices. The central purpose of the synagogue is worship and all synagogues contain an *ark*, which houses the scrolls or Torah. The ark usually has a curtain before it and an eternal light, or *Ne'er Tamud*, over the top. This light never goes out, reminding the Jew of God's everlasting presence. There will also be a reading desk which may be placed by the ark or in the centre of the building.

IMPORTANT FESTIVALS

In cyclical order the main Jewish festivals are:

Rosh Hashanah/New Year's Day

Rosh Hashanah commemorates the creation of the world. The blowing of the ram's horn (the shofar) reminds Jews of Abraham's sacrifice of a ram in place of his son. The symbol of the ram's horn has its origins in the concept of the scapegoat, which symbolically represented the sins of the people, which were driven out into the wilderness just as the goat was driven out from the community. This festival begins ten days of repentance and self examination during which God sits in judgement on each individual. On the eve of the festival apples are dipped in honey and distributed to the family and friends as a symbol for a sweet and happy New Year.

Yom Kippur

Yom Kippur is the last day of the ten days of repentance. This is the climax Day of Atonement and the holiest day of the year. Jews neither eat nor drink for a full day and spend a large part of the day in prayer, asking for forgiveness for past wrong-doing and resolving to improve in the following year.

Sukkot/Tabernacles

Sukkot is celebrated a few days after Yom Kippur. It is a harvest festival which also commemorates the forty years in the wilderness on the way from Egypt to Israel. Temporary huts are built and used during this festival for meals and other family activities. The open roof is covered with branches and decorated with fruit. This roofless hut, a Succoh, symbolises faith and dependence on God, and is a reminder of the Israelites wanderings in the wilderness where temporary huts were all they had to protect themselves. During the services held there, palm, myrtle and willow leaves together with citrus fruit are waved in all directions to symbolise that God can be found everywhere. At the end of the festival the Torah readings come to an end and the cycle starts again.

Simchat Torah

This festival immediately follows Sukkot, and is marked by great rejoicing. This celebrates the end of the annual cycle of reading the Torah and its immediate recommencement. All the scrolls of the Torah, are paraded seven times around the synagogue, followed by the children singing and dancing.

Hanukah/Festival of Lights

Hanukah celebrates both the Maccabean revolt – when Judas Maccabees and his followers refused to give up their faith despite persecution from the Graeco-Syrian oppressors – and the re-dedication of the Temple. A *Hanukyiah* (eight-branched candlestick) is used, one candle being lit on the first day, two on the second etc. An extra candle is used to light the others so the candlestick, or *menorah*, holds nine candles in all.

The eight candles remind Jews of the miracle of the small pot of oil, which was all that was available to relight the Temple lamp, which lasted for eight days.

Hanukah is a joyous festival with many happy traditions.

Purim

Purim is another joyful celebration. It commemorates the events of the book of Esther when the Jews in Persia were saved from a massacre planned by Haman. The biblical book of 'Esther' is read in the synagogue and when Haman's name is mentioned, the congregation armed with rattles and hooters erupts into noise to drown it out. Many people come in fancy dress and it is an occasion for parties and presents.

Pesach/Passover

Passover is one of the best known festivals and comes in the Spring. It marks the escape of the Jews from Egyptian slavery to freedom. The festival is rich in symbolism and ritual. The main focus is on

the symbolic meal (the *'seder'*) in the home with the telling of the Exodus story

and

the eating of unleavened bread (*Matzah*).

For the duration of the festival no food which contains yeast is eaten. Passover is a spring festival celebrating the barley harvest, and is called 'Firstfruits'. The overall significance of the festival is in the continuity of Judaism.

Shavuot/Pentecost

Pentecost is another harvest festival celebrated seven weeks after Passover. It also commemorates the giving of the Law to Moses.

Tisha B'Av/The Ninth of Av

This festival is a full day fast, mourning the destruction of the First Temple (built by King Solomon in Jerusalem) by the Babylonians in 586 BCE and of the Second Temple (Herod's Temple) by the Romans in 70 CE.

IMPORTANT RELIGIOUS PRACTICES

Judaism is rich in symbolism and ritual practice.

Worship and Prayer

Worship takes place in home and Synagogue. In the orthodox tradition the man takes the dominant place and women have no part in the service, except on the Sabbath (Saturday). In the liberal/progressive movement women are included in all aspects of the religion.

Prayers are usually in Hebrew, but English (or the particular national language) is sometimes used. The prayer book (*Siddur*) has an important role in Jewish religious practice, and contains prayers for all occasions. There are special prayers for special occasions to remind Jews of God's goodness and blessing. Prayers should be said three times a day with sincerity and belief. Men cover their heads with a cap (*Yarmulka*) and wear a prayer shawl (*Tallit*). On the ordinary days of the week *Tefillin* (also called *Phylacteries*) may be put on the arm and head. These are two small cubic boxes of black leather which are fastened by straps, one to the head and the other to the left arm. They contain biblical texts written on parchment and are worn by men for the recitation of morning prayers. Prayers are normally said standing and facing Jerusalem.

Pilgrimage

Jews are not obliged by the rules of their faith to go on pilgrimage. However for centuries Jerusalem has been the focal point for pilgrims. Jerusalem is the Jewish holy city and centre of Judaism.

Food Laws

Food plays an important part in Jewish life. There are many laws concerning food based on the Book of Leviticus. Only animals which have cloven hooves and chew the cud may be eaten. Fish with fins and scales are acceptable and birds which eat seeds. Religiously acceptable food is known as *Kosher*. In addition, meat and milk products cannot be eaten together which means, for example, butter may not be used on meat sandwiches. Animals must also be killed in a humane and ritual way.

Rites of Passage

During their early years the first important prayer a Jewish child learns is the *Shema* – the Jewish affirmation of belief (Deuteronomy 6⁴). The Shema begins with the famous words, given to the Jewish people by the prophet Moses, 'Hear, O Israel, the Lord our God is one Lord; and you shall love the

Lord your God with all your heart, and with all your soul, and with all your might'.

Circumcision

In Judaism boys are circumcised at eight days of age to commemorate Abraham's covenant with God.

Bar-Mitzvah

At the age of thirteen a boy becomes *Bar-Mitzvah* (son of the commandment); on the Sabbath after his birthday he reads from the scroll of the Torah during the synagogue service for the first time. After the service there is usually a party for family and friends. From this point on he is regarded as a responsible person. He is expected to fulfil all the duties of a Jew. A Jewish girl automatically comes of age at twelve and is considered to be 'Bar-Mitzvah' (daughter of the commandment). In some synagogues it is the custom to hold a ceremony to mark the occasion.

Marriage

In Judaism marriage is considered to be a holy covenant. Before the ceremony the bridegroom signs the marriage document (*Ketubbah*) in which he pledges himself to his bride. During the ceremony the couple stand under an embroidered canopy (*chuppah*) supported by four poles, which symbolises their future home. The ceremony ends with the breaking of a glass under the bridegroom's foot. This symbolic act is usually considered to have two interpretations: one concerning the couple themselves and their need to be aware of pain as well as the great joy of the ceremony; and the other a symbolic reminder of the destruction of the temple of Jerusalem, a theme constantly reappearing in Jewish rituals and prayers. The traditional greeting 'muzeltof' (meaning congratulations) is used after the ceremony.

Death

The final words Jews should say, or have said for them, are the words of the Shema. The funeral service, which is characterised by simplicity, no matter how rich the deceased, is arranged as soon as possible, preferably within twenty four hours of the death. No prayers for the dead are offered but *kaddish*, a prayer of praise to God, is recited in their memory. It is the particular responsibility of the son to say kaddish on behalf of a deceased parent.

After the funeral the close relatives return home for a week of private mourning. This period is known as *shivah*, or the seven days. As a sign of grief the mourners sit on low stools, or on the floor. On the anniversary of the parent's death, the children light a memorial candle and recite the kaddish at the end of the synagogue service.

JUDAISM

For further reading:

Steinberg, M.	BASIC JUDAISM	Harvest 1947
Marmur, D.	BEYOND SURVIVAL	D.L.T. 1982
	JEWISH HISTORY ATLAS	Martin Gilbert
Blue, L.	A BACKDOOR TO HEAVEN	D.L.T.
	FORMS OF PRAYER	R.S.G.B.
Goldberg and Rayner	JUDAISM	Penguin
Trepp, L.	JUDAISM, DEVELOPMENT & LIFE	Dickenson

BUDDHISM

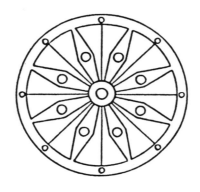

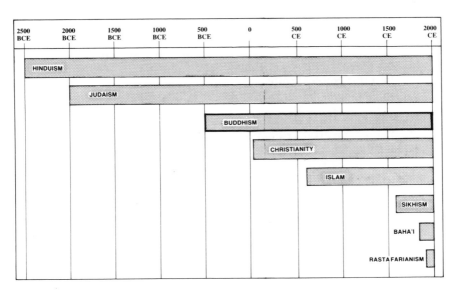

2500 BCE	2000 BCE	1500 BCE	1000 BCE	500 BCE	0	500 CE	1000 CE	1500 CE	2000 CE

HINDUISM

JUDAISM

BUDDHISM

CHRISTIANITY

ISLAM

SIKHISM

BAHA'I

RASTAFARIANISM

BUDDHISM

ORIGINS

Buddhism has its roots in India around 2,500 years ago. The founder of Buddhism was an Indian Hindu prince, *Siddhartha Gautama*, who became known as 'the Buddha' i.e. 'the Enlightened One'. The Buddha's teachings are explored in greater detail in the next two sections, however the heart of the *Dharma* (teachings) concerns the Four Noble Truths and the Eightfold Path. It is in the interpretation of Dharma that the two main branches of Buddhism emerged after the death of Buddha. The *Theravada* i.e. 'the doctrine of the elders' is the strict conservative branch of Buddhism; in contrast are the more liberal Mahasanghikas i.e. 'the members of the great community'. The Mahasanghikas chose for their school of thought the name *Mahayana*, meaning 'great vehicle'. According to the Mahayana tradition of Buddhism salvation is not intended for a few people of particular moral excellence as Theravada tradition demands, but for all mankind. Many other branches of Buddhism have emerged from the Buddha's original teachings.

BASIC BELIEFS

The main Buddhist beliefs can be divided into three key areas:
    i   the Three Universal Truths
    ii the Four Noble Truths
    iii the Eightfold Path.

i The Three Universal Truths

The Three Universal Truths comprise the concepts defined in the terms *anicca*, *dukkha* and *anatta*.

1 – *Anicca* is the term for the impermanence and changeability which marks all existence. There is therefore no rest in the world, and everything is subject to change:

2 – *Dukkha* is the term for suffering or unsatisfactoriness. All aspects of life include suffering, and Buddha's teaching seeks to overcome suffering by using wisdom, and through wisdom to find one's true nature and reach *nirvana*, the ultimate goal of life:

3 – *Anatta* is the term indicating that there is ultimately no 'soul'. The Buddha taught that all beings are merely a series of mental and physical states. This was a development of, and a conflict with, the

Hindu doctrine of reincarnation. Buddha's teaching on the Three Universal Truths also involved the key concept of karma.

Karma, originally a Hindu concept, is the law of cause and effect. Karma operates in both the moral and physical dimensions of human life. Buddha taught that people were reborn into a new life when they died. Life, for Buddhists, is an endless round of existence – being born, dying and being reborn. This is called the *Samsara* cycle, and in order to be free from this cycle Buddhists seek to reach nirvana, when karma no longer affects them. Until nirvana is achieved Buddha taught that through reincarnation or rebirth all human beings reap good or evil consequences of their actions. The quality of their deeds, their speech and their thought in previous lives determines the circumstances of their rebirth. By a proper understanding of the human situation i.e. the imprisonment in the process of karma, and by obedience to the right conditions, it is possible to transcend the human situation. This means not the abolition of karma, but liberation into a new process, a 'good karma', where its good effects are experienced in oneself and others. The process, Buddha taught, involved acceptance of the Four Noble Truths and the Eightfold Path.

ii **Four Noble Truths**

These Truths are central to Buddha's teachings. Buddha explained that if the Truths are understood and then accepted, the way to new life is open to all.

1   *Suffering is part of life*
    The first Truth is that the universal human experience of suffering, mental and emotional as well as physical, is the effect of past karma.

2   *Suffering is due to selfish desires*
    The second Truth is the perception that the cause of such suffering is craving or desiring the wrong things. Buddha taught that nothing in the material world is worthy of reverence, or can be depended upon, therefore to desire would bring suffering.

3   *Suffering will stop if desires are crushed*
    The third Truth is that it is possible for suffering to cease through avoidance of desire.

4   *The way to crush desire is through following the Noble Eightfold Path*
    The fourth Truth says that there is a way of escaping from suffering in this world and so entering the state of nirvana. The solution is the Eightfold Path, which Buddha described as the signposts to a right life-style.

iii **The Eightfold Path** is described by Buddha as:

1 *Right knowledge*, or understanding, or belief in the Four Noble Truths;

2 *Right attitude*, or thought, or resolve indicating a mental attitude of goodwill, peaceableness, keeping far from oneself all sensual desire, hate and malice;

3 *Right speech* where speech must be wise, truthful and directed towards reconciliation;

4 *Right action* which embraces all moral behaviour – especially forbidden are murder, stealing, adultery and abuse of people;

5 *Right occupation*, or livelihood where one's way of earning a living must not be harmful to others;

6 *Right effort* where noble thoughts, words and deeds may be nurtured and developed; getting rid of evil influences and seeking good works;

7 *Right mindfulness*, means careful consideration, not giving in to the dictates of desire in thought, speech, action and emotions;

8 *Right composure*, or concentration; to meditate with single-mindedness of purpose and therefore train the mind to the perfection of concentration needed for a person to enter nirvana.

Symbolically the Eightfold Path is represented by the eight spokes in the Buddhist Wheel of Life.

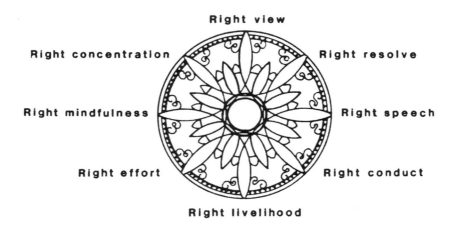

Right view

Right concentration

Right resolve

Right mindfulness

Right speech

Right effort

Right conduct

Right livelihood

Essentially the Eightfold Path is concerned with –

> morality (right speech; right action; right occupation);
> spirituality (right effort; right mindfulness; right composure);
> insight (right knowledge; right attitude).

Two final concepts are essential to the basic beliefs of Buddhism – nirvana and dharma.

Nirvana – The goal of life for a Buddhist is nirvana. Nirvana is the transformed mode of human consciousness which is also an independent reality with a dynamism of its own. Nirvana, meaning 'going out', is the release from karma, where suffering ceases because the desires have been controlled.

Dharma – Dharma is the way to the goal of nirvana. The Buddha spoke of dharma as 'lovely', and taught that the essence of the religious life 'consists in friendship, in association, in intimacy with what is lovely'. Friendship with the 'lovely' is the prior condition for both the beginning and the sustained practice of the Noble Eightfold Path.

IMPORTANT PEOPLE:

Siddhartha Gautama – founder of Buddhism

Gautama, who came to be called the Buddha, and founder of Buddhism, was born about 560 BCE in a village called Lumbini, near the modern border between India and Nepal. His father was a local rajah, and Gautama lived a life of ease and luxury in their palace. Gautama however was driven by an inner compulsion to leave this outwardly splendid existence for the homeless life of a holy man. This was very much in the Hindu religious tradition at that time, and Northern India at Gautama's time was one of the world's great centres of intellectual and spiritual activity. Gautama's decision to become a holy man was evidently the result of a long felt aspiration to higher spiritual fulfilment. He took instruction from religious teachers but grew increasingly dissatisfied with the severe asceticism of the Hindu tradition.

The key turning point prior to his enlightenment was his realisation of the spiritual and moral futility of that extreme asceticism. Gautama adopted methods of meditation and faith that were to be instrumental in his enlightenment, and became an essential feature in the Buddhist religious tradition. The Buddha, as he was now called after his enlightenment, began to teach and soon won many disciples. Buddha was tempted to stay under his famous Bodhi-tree at Bodh-Gaya, but he decided that this new knowledge he had gained should be passed on to others.

Buddha preached his famous sermons from Deer Park at Benares, a traditionally holy place for Hindus. His first sermon outlined his teachings which included the first statement of the Four Noble Truths and the Eightfold Path. The Buddha then travelled around Northern India for the next forty-five years teaching. A group of disciples followed him, and the first Buddhist community (*Sangha*) was established.

When Buddha died in 480 BCE, aged eighty, his teaching had been widely accepted and the Sangha was an established community throughout Northern India.

Emperor Asoka – 270–232 BCE

Asoka was a famous Indian King who inherited an empire in northern India. Asoka renounced Brahminical Hindu statecraft because it required him to pursue an imperialist policy and became a Buddhist lay follower. He encouraged the spread of Buddhist teaching throughout India. He showed by example many of the basic Buddhist teachings. He forbade the taking of human and animal life. He showed concern for the welfare of his people by establishing hospitals, hostels, new wells and many plantations. He had edicts of Buddhist statecraft inscribed on rocks and pillars throughout his country. More importantly he made Buddhism much more attractive to ordinary people.

During his reign Asoka gathered together the foremost Buddhist monks and teachers from all around Southern Asia to compile texts of Buddhist thought and teaching.

IMPORTANT BOOKS

In 253 BCE, nearly 200 years after the Buddha's death, Emperor Asoka organised a meeting of Buddhist monks at Pataliputta to classify Buddhist traditions and teachings into an organised form. This was the third such council since Buddha's death, and all teachings were still in an oral form. It was not until the first century BCE, on what is now Sri Lanka, that the first Buddhist scriptures were written down.

This basic collection of writings, or canon, is called the *Pali* canon, after the language in which it is written. The Pali canon is more popularly called the *Tripitaka*, meaning 'three baskets' because it is in three parts:

Vinaya – pitaka, the basket of order, which gives the monks guidance on discipline for life;

Sutta – pitaka, the basket of teachings, which contains the Buddha's teachings, and is the most important part;

Abhidhamma – pitaka, the basket of higher teaching, for intellectual, academic treatises on Buddhism.

In addition to the Pali canon, there are many other important Buddhist writings in Pali, Sanskrit, Chinese and other Asian languages.

Both Theravada and Mahayana Buddhists accept the Tripitaka as their sacred writings, however the Mahayanas also recognise many more texts as authoritative. The *Sutras* are an important example of such texts. The most important of the Sutras are the Diamond Scripture and the Lotus Scripture. The lotus itself is a symbol of the Buddha and his teaching. These sutras introduce a vital concept to the Mahayana tradition i.e. *bodhisattvas* ('Buddhas-to-be'), which is not accepted by the Theravadans. Many of the sutras aim to give practical guidance to worship, others are more intellectual in nature. Whole schools of thought gather around the sutras, and then write their own teaching books (*shastras*), to give a thorough insight and interpretation of the sacred writings.

IMPORTANT BUILDINGS

Monasteries

Monasteries are at the centre of Buddhist life. The Sangha (Buddhist community) lives in the monastery, although these are not closed communities just for the monks. The ordinary lay Buddhists take an active role in the Sangha by visiting the monasteries for worship or study. Within the larger monasteries the monks are often self sufficient for food.

The most important, and often most beautiful building is the shrine which always faces east. Within the shrine there is always a Buddha figure, and often a relic of some Buddhist holy person or even the Buddha himself.

The monastery often has a building which serves as a school, where local children can attend in order to learn reading and writing.

Shrines and Temples

Buddhist shrines and temples are built to symbolise the Five Elements of the faith i.e. earth, fire, air, water and wisdom. Each Element has a symbolic representation which is present in the structural appearance of the temple or shrine. These symbols are arranged vertically beginning from the base with a square (symbol for earth), followed by an oval (air symbol), a circle (fire symbol), a horizontal line (water symbol) and finally a vertical line, representing wisdom.

Shrines and temples are centres of Buddhist social life, not just places of worship. Many shrines and temples contain fine examples of religious architecture and paintings and sculptures of the highest quality.

IMPORTANT FESTIVALS
in cyclical order

Wesak or Vaisakha Puja

Wesak is the most important festival in the Buddhist calendar. Theravada Buddhists celebrate the birth, enlightenment and death of Gautama Buddha on this day. Mahayana Buddhists have separate days to celebrate each of them. Houses are decorated with lanterns and garlands and in many countries captive birds are released to symbolise Buddha's compassion. The particular emphasis of the day is on Buddha's enlightenment.

Poson or Dhamma Vijaya

Poson is a Theravada festival which celebrates the first preaching of Buddhist doctrine outside India, particularly in Sri Lanka.

Obon

This Mahayana festival is celebrated by Japanese Buddhists. It is a time of remembering family ancestors. They are welcomed back home with feasting and dancing. Fires are also lit to light their arrival and departure. A similar Chinese Buddhist festival in September is called 'Lost Souls' or 'All Souls Day'.

Asala or Dhammacakka Day

This festival of the 'turning of the Wheel of the Law' is a Theravada celebration of the First Proclamation by Gautama Buddha in the Deer Park, near Benares. The Proclamation taught the Noble Eightfold Path and the Four Noble Truths.

Higan or Shuban No Hi

This Mahayana festival marks the autumn equinox. As at the spring equinox, harmony and balance are the themes, sutras are recited and the graves of relatives are visited.

Omisoka

Omisoka is a Japanese festival during which preparations for the new year are made by cleansing home shrines and altars. The bells of Buddhist temples are struck 108 times to warn against the 108 evils to be overcome.

Ganjitsu

New Year's Day is celebrated in various ways in different countries. Usually there are parades and in shrines the images of Buddha are ceremonially bathed.

Magha Puja

This festival at the full moon is a celebration to remember the occasion when Buddha laid down the rules for Buddhist monks.

Hana Matsuri

This flower festival marks the Japanese celebration of the birth of the Buddha, which Mahayanas fix in 565 BCE. Tradition has it that the Buddha was born in a garden, so floral shrines are made and an image of the infant Buddha is set in each shrine and bathed.

IMPORTANT RELIGIOUS PRACTICES

Worship and Prayer

Individual worship may be carried out in the temple shrine or in the shrine at home. Many Buddhists may meditate rather than pray, as the Buddha taught that prayer was unnecessary because there is no 'One' to pray to.

Collective worship is at a monastery, or shrine or temple. People take off their shoes before entering, then go and sit on mats facing the image of Buddha. Worship is silent as, in general, people meditate on the Buddha's teaching and example. In worship Buddhists perform the anjali i.e. they place the palms of their hands together before their forehead and then stretch them up towards the Buddha's image. Next they will prostrate three times in honour of the Buddha, the Dharma and the Sangha. Offerings of flowers and lighted candles are made. One of the most important acts of worship is meditation.

Meditation

The Buddha himself demonstrated the importance of meditation since he presented a clear outline of meditation in the last three stages of the Eightfold Path i.e. right effort, right mindfulness and right composure. Buddha taught that the purpose of meditation is to help achieve enlightenment and eventually nirvana. A key sacred formula called the Three Refuges is often spoken, or may be chanted regularly during meditation. The three Refuges are also the initial initiation into Buddhism and say

'I go to the Buddha for refuge;
I go to the Dharma for refuge;
I go to the Sangha for refuge.'

Pilgrimage

Buddhists have a number of special places which have become centres of pilgrimage. Many of these places are closely associated with the life of the Buddha in some way e.g. at Bodh-Gaya where Buddha sat under the Bo Tree and became enlightened. When Buddha died and was cremated some of his remains (called relics) were sent to various Buddhist centres where shrines were built to house them. One of the most famous is the Temple of the Sacred Tooth at Kandy in Sri Lanka.

RITES OF PASSAGE

Initiation

To become a Buddhist there is no special ceremony needed, only the sincere repetition of the sacred formula, 'the Three Refuges'. After this acceptance of the Buddha's teaching it is then a matter of putting that faith into practice.

To become a Buddhist monk however there is a ceremony involving the *naag* (the name given to a person seeking to become a monk), the abbot (head of the monastery) and the *Sangha* (the community of monks). Before initiation the naag must shave off all hair on the head and answer questions from the elder monks. If the answers are satisfactory, and none of the monks object, the naag is admitted to the Sangha and his religious training begins.

All monks must observe ten rules which guide them in their everyday living. The first five are also applicable to all Buddhists, and are known as the 'Five Precepts'. The remaining five apply only to monks. These rules state that they: must not take the life of any living creature;

must not steal anyone's possessions;

must not be involved in sexual misconduct;

must not tell any lies;

must not use any alcohol or misuse drugs;

must not eat after midday;

must not attend shows where there is music or dancing;

must not use any perfume or personal jewellery;

must not sleep on raised or upholstered beds;

must not accept gifts of gold or silver.

Marriage

There is no religious wedding ceremony in the temple or monastery; instead a simple ceremony takes place in the home. The bride and groom exchange vows promising to honour and respect each other. Sometimes a monk may attend and will tie the thumbs of the groom and the bride with ceremonial thread to symbolise their unity. At a later stage the bride and groom will visit the monastery to receive the monks' blessing and hear a sermon of the Buddha's teaching about married life.

Funerals

Buddhists may be buried or cremated. At the place of burial the monks will recite the Three Refuges and the Five Precepts. The relatives perform the symbolic actions of giving the white cloth which covers the coffin to the monks, who are asked to share their merit with the deceased; and the mourners pour water into a cup until it overflows, symbolising the transfer of merit to the deceased. The monks will then recite suitable verses from Buddhist scripture and give a sermon on life and death.

BUDDHISM

For further reading:

de Bary, W. T.	THE BUDDHIST TRADITION	Vintage
Ling, T.	THE BUDDHA	Penguin
Rapula, W.	WHAT THE BUDDHA TAUGHT	Gordon Fraser
Robinson, R.	THE BUDDHIST RELIGION	Dickenson
Saddhatissa, H.	THE BUDDHA'S WAY	Allen & Unwin
Saddhatissa, H.	THE LIFE OF THE BUDDHA	Allen & Unwin
Schumann, H.	BUDDHISM	Rider

CHRISTIANITY

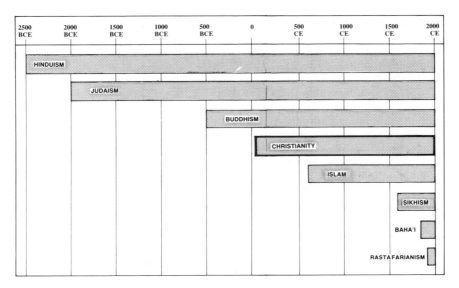

2500 BCE	2000 BCE	1500 BCE	1000 BCE	500 BCE	0	500 CE	1000 CE	1500 CE	2000 CE

HINDUISM

JUDAISM

BUDDHISM

CHRISTIANITY

ISLAM

SIKHISM

BAHA'I

RASTAFARIANISM

CHRISTIANITY

ORIGINS

Christianity has its origins in the tradition of Judaism. It centres around the person of Jesus of Nazareth who was born a Jew around the year 4 BCE, in the land now called Israel. Christian belief that Jesus was not only a historical figure but also the Christ, the Son of God, gives Christianity both a historical and a spiritual base.

At the time of Jesus, the Jews were a subject people of the Roman Empire. The Jews were looking for the coming of the Messiah (meaning 'the anointed one') spoken of by their prophets, who they believed would free them from the foreign rule of the Romans and set up 'God's kingdom on earth'. Around 27 CE, John the Baptist began preaching about the Messiah who would be coming soon. Some Jews saw the Messiah in more spiritual terms as a priest-prophet, but the popular expectation amongst Jews was that of a political Messiah – a liberator from Roman rule. Christians believe that Jesus of Nazareth was the expected Messiah.

BASIC BELIEFS

At the time of Jesus, the sacred writings of the Jews set out the principal beliefs which were later to be incorporated into basic Christian beliefs:

Jewish belief in monotheism i.e. in the existence of one God, the Creator and Lord of the Universe, who is above all mankind;

Jewish belief in mankind as the image of God, but having rebelled against the Creator;

Jewish belief that God, as well as judge is also merciful; God would provide mankind with the rules by which mankind could save themselves;

Jewish belief that God had revealed himself to the Israelites and they were the chosen people of God;

Jewish belief that God would send the Messiah to rule over the chosen people, and they would be set free from their enemies for ever;

Jewish belief that God, through the guidance of the law given in the Torah, would set out how to live the right life and through this salvation would be found.

Christians believe that Jesus was the expected Messiah. It is the rejection of this belief by Jews that constitutes the decisive difference between Judaism and Christianity.

The development of essentially Christian belief is reflected in the two principal creeds of Christianity: the Apostles' Creed and the Nicene Creed. These can be summarised thus:

Christian belief that God exists and is the supreme being, the creator of all;

Christian belief that Jesus was a man and also the son of God;

Christian belief that God sent Jesus to save mankind and this could only be accomplished by Jesus' death on the cross and his resurrection;

Christian belief that Jesus is in heaven with God and that at some future time God will judge all mankind according to their actions and beliefs during their lives;

Christian belief that God is present in the world through the Holy Spirit;

Christian belief that individuals can be saved i.e. forgiven their sins, and thus experience eternal life here and now – a spiritual relationship with God which transcends physical death.

Christians therefore believe Jesus to be more than just an important prophet. The early Christian would have affirmed that 'Jesus Christ is Lord'. The special relationship between Jesus and God is described in the creeds as that between son and father. Christians express this belief by referring to Jesus as the Son of God.

IMPORTANT PEOPLE

Jesus of Nazareth

Jesus was born around the year 4 BCE. His birthplace is traditionally held to be Bethlehem in Judea. Jesus was a Jew and lived most of his life in Galilee. Christians claim that their belief that Jesus was truly human but also uniquely the son of God, is supported by the extraordinary events recorded in the birth narratives found in the gospels of Matthew and Luke.

Very little is known of Jesus' life from an infant to the age of about thirty. The event which first brought him into public prominence was the mission of his cousin John 'the Baptist'. John called on the Jews to return to God, and baptised in the River Jordan all those who responded to his call to repentance. Jesus then left his settled life in Nazareth and made his way to Judea where he also was baptised by John. Jesus now believed that it was time to begin the work God had given him to do. Gathering twelve special disciples from amongst those who were challenged by his message, he began his activities.

The gospels summarise Jesus' activities as 'preaching, teaching and healing'. Jesus became a well-known figure in Galilee over the following two or three years. On many occasions he challenged the authority of the ruling Jewish religious leaders. At Passover time Jesus went to Jerusalem with his disciples. He had directly challenged the Jewish religious leaders in Jerusalem by driving the traders and money-lenders out of the courtyard of the Temple, as he considered they were defiling God's house. Furthermore, these leaders felt threatened by Jesus' growing popularity. Eventually they arrested him with the help of Judas, one of his disciples. Jesus was tried according to Jewish law on a charge of blasphemy, because it was alleged that he claimed to be the Messiah and the son of God. A death sentence was passed, but a Roman conviction was needed to make it effective. This was secured by a charge of sedition, forced upon the unwilling Roman governor, Pilate, by the religious leaders in Jerusalem, with popular local support. So, ironically, the Jesus who had forfeited his popularity by his refusal to take up direct arms against Rome, was put to death on a cross by Rome as a political rebel. The cross has become the symbol of Christianity.

The gospels go on to record that God raised Jesus from the dead and that he appeared to his followers on several occasions. Finally he met them on the Mount of Olives and after giving them instructions to preach the gospel 'to the ends of the earth', he left them and as the gospels state was taken from their sight. The Acts of the Apostles tells that a few days later at the feast of Pentecost the disciples were filled with the Holy Spirit, as Jesus had promised, and from that time onwards they went out to preach the message of the gospel.

Peter

Simon Peter, one of the original twelve disciples of Jesus, became the leader of the Jerusalem community of followers in the early Church. He travelled to Rome and is said to have been put to death there in about 67 CE during a period of persecution of Christians by the Emperor. Tradition has it that Peter was crucified upside-down. Peter is known as the first Bishop of Rome, and the Roman Catholic Church maintains that each bishop of Rome (Pope) stands in direct succession from St. Peter, and that he continues the task of St. Peter in providing a kind of final authority as Christ's representative on earth.

Paul

Paul was the key figure in the growth and expansion of the early Christian Church. He was a Jew and a Roman citizen, and was active in the persecution of Christians. But, after a vision on the road to Damascus, he was converted to the Christian faith. His subsequent missionary journeys were instrumental in spreading Christianity beyond the Jewish community to towns and cities all over the Roman Empire. Paul's writings form a major part of the New Testament.

IMPORTANT BOOKS

The Christian holy book is the Bible. Many Christians call the contents of the book 'the Word of God' since they believe that through the Bible God speaks to his people. Christians believe that the Bible contains various accounts of how the Jews and the early Christians believed that God was at work in their lives, both as individuals and as a nation, seeking to fulfil his purpose for mankind.

The word 'Bible' comes from the Greek 'biblia' meaning 'the books'. The plural form indicates the nature of the Bible. The Bible is a collection of books written over a period of more than a thousand years, in a wide variety of cultural, historical and linguistic situations.

The Bible is divided into two parts: the Old Testament and the New Testament. The word 'testament' comes from the concept of 'covenant' or 'agreement'.

The Old Testament is basically the Hebrew scriptures of Judaism. They present the history and religious thought of the people of God, the 'chosen' people, up to the time of Jesus. The books also show how, over the centuries, God's prophets revealed more of God's nature. In the Old Testament there are thirty-nine books covering different areas of scripture including laws, history, stories, poetry, wisdom and prophecy.

The New Testament contains twenty-seven books comprising gospels (accounts of, and reflection upon) the life and works of Jesus; history (the development of the early Church); letters (written by leaders of the early Church to newly developing Christian communities); and the Revelation of St. John the Divine (an account of a visionary experience).

The Bible is of vital importance for the Christian faith. It is used in both public and private worship. In theory, therefore, all Christians accept it as authoritative, both in guiding their actions and informing their beliefs. In practice, however, Christians have differed in their use and interpretation of the Bible.

IMPORTANT BUILDINGS

The general name for a Christian building for worship is a church. This word comes from the Greek meaning 'Lord's House'. However, not all Christian groups worship in a church; there are Meeting Houses (Quaker), Citadels (Salvation Army), Chapels – and other terms are also used.

In Britain churches may be of various denominations including:

Church of England, Church of Scotland, Church of Wales, or Church of Ireland;

Roman Catholic;

Pentecostalist, Methodist, Baptist, United Reformed.

One of the main features of most parish churches is the cross-shaped interior which symbolises the death and resurrection of Jesus Christ. Inside the church, the *altar* is usually the focal point of the building.

In Roman Catholic churches one distinctive feature is the *confession boxes* where, in privacy, people confess their sins to the priest and seek God's forgiveness through him.

In Free Churches, the preaching of God's word is generally considered the most important part of worship, so the *pulpit* occupies a prominent place at the front of the church.

A Cathedral is a very large church which contains the throne, or *'cathedra'* of the bishop of the *diocese* (the extent of a bishop's jurisdiction, which is usually divided into parishes).

IMPORTANT FESTIVALS

The following festivals and seasons are particularly important in the calendar of the Christian church:

Advent

The Christian year begins with a period of preparation for Christmas, which reminds Christians of both the birth of Jesus (and the Incarnation) and the Second Coming of Jesus (at the end of the world).

Christmas

25th December is the day assigned by the early Church for the joyful celebration and commemoration of Jesus' birth.

Lent

The forty day preparation period prior to Easter. It corresponds to the forty days Jesus spent fasting in the wilderness before beginning his preaching and teaching in public.

Good Friday

The solemn memorial of the death of Jesus by crucifixion.

Easter

The most important Christian festival, celebrating the resurrection of Jesus.

The week leading up to Easter Sunday is called 'Holy Week' and is in March or April each year.

Ascension Day

The celebration, on the fortieth day after Easter, of Jesus' ascension into heaven.

Pentecost

Named after the Jewish Festival on which the followers (apostles) of Jesus Christ first received the Holy Spirit and proclaimed the Gospel. It is often thought of as the birthday of the church. The alternative name Whitsun derives from the custom of converts presenting themselves for baptism dressed in white on this day (Whit Sunday).

The whole Christian year revolves around the historical events in the life of Jesus and events concerning the early Church and its teaching. All the above festivals are celebrated in church with special services when appropriate passages from the Bible are read, prayers, are said and hymns are sung on themes related to the particular festival.

IMPORTANT RELIGIOUS PRACTICES

Worship

The Christian holy day is Sunday. The gospels record that Jesus was raised from the dead on the day after the Jewish Sabbath. Therefore Sunday is symbolic to Christians, as they are reminded on that day of the resurrection of Jesus.

Christian churches, and individual Christians, have many distinctive ways of worshipping God, but in most forms of worship common elements occur such as the singing of hymns or psalms, the reading or reciting of prayers, Bible readings, and the preaching of sermons. Historically the Early Church introduced a pattern of worship that is still reflected today. The early believers gathered for the apostles' teaching, for prayer, for fellowship, and particularly for the 'breaking of bread'. The Lord's Supper (also known as Holy Communion or Eucharist) was, and is, a central act of Christian worship for most denominations. For many Christians Holy Communion is probably the most important act of worship. It celebrates, symbolises and re-enacts the 'Last Supper', which was the final meal Jesus had with his disciples before his crucifixion. The sharing of bread, and sometimes wine, is a symbolic act by priest and people.

Different Christian groups emphasise different ways of worship, for example, the celebration of Mass in the Roman Catholic Church, the preaching of God's Word in the Free Churches, and the silence in the Quaker meeting. The pattern for services of worship is usually written out in special books e.g. in the Church of England the Book of Common Prayer or the new Alternative Service Book; in the Roman Catholic Church the Missal book; in the Methodist Church the New Service Book.

Prayer

Prayer – communication with God – is essential to the Christian life. Christians use different kinds of prayer e.g. adoration (praising God); confession (asking God to forgive sins); thanksgiving (gratitude to God for all things in life); and supplication (asking God for help and guidance).

The best known example of Christian prayer is the Lord's Prayer. This was the prayer Jesus taught the disciples. It has become a pattern for Christian prayer throughout the ages.

Christians today are concerned with relating prayer to life at many points. The impact of a more secular life has led many Christians to look for more meaningful ways of talking about God. Prayer is seen not as withdrawal from the world but as involvement in it, at all levels from individual to political.

Pilgrimage

Pilgrimage is a journey to a holy place, undertaken as a commemoration of a past event, as a celebration, or as an act of penance. For Christians there are many places which fall into those categories of pilgrimage. Traditionally the Holy Land, i.e. present day Israel, is a place of pilgrimage. Pilgrims visit the places where Jesus lived, worked and died. Christians also make pilgrimages to places associated with the lives of important Christian saints, or important places where visions have been reported.

Examples of such pilgrimages include:

Rome – many asssociations with the Early Church and present Roman Catholic Church, e.g. the Vatican Palace (home of the Pope); St. Peter's Basilica

Canterbury Cathedral – shrine of the famous martyr St. Thomas a Becket; the Archbishop of Canterbury is the spiritual leader of the Anglican Communion.

Walsingham, in Norfolk – site of the 11th Century shrine to the Virgin Mary; now two modern shrines exist – one Anglican and one Roman Catholic.

Durham Cathedral – site of St. Cuthbert's tomb.

Holy Island (Lindisfarne) – base of St. Aidan, a famous missionary.

Iona – St. Columba's base in Scotland.

Downpatric, Ireland – St. Patrick's tomb; Knock, Ireland – visions of the Virgin Mary reported.

Lourdes, France – St. Bernadette reported visions of the Virgin Mary, and where many believe that the water from a certain spring has miraculous powers.

Food and Fasting

Christians use bread and wine as symbols of Jesus' body and blood. The symbolic sharing of these foods by Christians commemorates and celebrates the death and resurrection of Jesus Christ.

The period of Lent has always been associated with fasting. Lent reminds Christians of the time when Jesus spent forty days fasting in the desert. For Christians Lent can be a period of fasting, meditation and penance. In this way Christians prepare for the most important festival of Easter.

Clothes

Clothes have particular significance for the Christian clergy i.e. priest, minister or elder, in that certain garments have particular significance for certain occasions. This may be reflected in what is worn, or the particular colour of clothes. Traditionally certain clothes and colours are associated with Christian ceremonies e.g. white dress for a bride at a wedding; black tie for mourners at a funeral.

Rites of Passage and Sacraments

Rites of passage are specific, and usually symbolic, ceremonies which mark the transition from one state of religious development to another. Examples in the Christian faith are concerned mainly with birth rites, initiation rites, marriage rites and funeral rites. In some Christian denominations rites are regarded as sacraments. These sacraments represent an outward and visible sign of an inward and spiritual religious development. For Roman Catholic, Orthodox, and C. of E. Churches, baptism, confirmation and eucharist, marriage, ordination, penance and holy unction (the anointing of the sick by a priest) are sacraments, whereas in some other churches baptism and the eucharist are the only rites regarded as sacraments.

Baptism

Baptism is the sacrament of entry into the Christian church. The ceremony is conducted by a priest or a minister. Washing in water in the name of the Christian trinity (i.e. God – Father, Son and Holy Spirit), symbolises the person's identification with Jesus Christ's death and resurrection, in dying and being raised to new life. Usually baptism takes place within months of a baby being born, in which case baptism may be the forerunner to the child's later confirmation. Baptism can, however, be a solely adult ceremony either for people 'converting', or taking on Christian beliefs in adult life; or in the case of the Baptist Church, baptism takes place when a person is of an age to understand fully the meaning of the Christian faith, and is ready to accept all the responsibilities and duties of a church member.

Confirmation

Confirmation is the rite involving the laying on of hands, by a senior churchperson such as a bishop, on those who have been baptised, with a prayer for the gift of, or strengthening by, the Holy Spirit. Confirmation is often the sign of becoming a communicant member of the church. In Orthodox Churches it is performed at baptism. In the Roman Catholic church children are usually confirmed from ten years old, after their First Communion which is at 7–8 years old. Other Churches which accept confirmation usually offer it from about the age of twelve upwards.

Eucharist

Eucharist, meaning 'Thanksgiving', is the central act of Christian worship, instituted by Jesus Christ on the night before his death. The eucharist involves the sharing of bread (and sometimes wine) which are sacramentally associated with the body and blood of Jesus Christ.

Marriage

Marriage is a legal contract made between two people, which can if the couple wish also become a religious rite. In Christianity it is not essential to be married in church, a legal ceremony can take place in a register office, conducted by the local registrar; however the traditional Christian marriage takes place as a wedding rite in a church, conducted by a priest or a minister. The wedding ceremony has an important religious significance as it is the agreed union of a couple seeking God's blessing through the church.

Ordination

Ordination is the rite in the Christian church by which men (and, in some churches, women) are authorised as minister of the church, through which they become God's servants, and perform spiritual functions for their congregations, for example, administering sacraments and preaching. In the Roman Catholic churches priests must be male and celibate.

Penance

Penance is the rite where Christians ask God for forgiveness, and perform some act of acknowledgement for their sins i.e. wrongdoings. Penance may be the saying of prayers, or the undertaking of duties within the church community, as recommended by the priest. In the Roman Catholic, Orthodox and Anglican Churches penance has a formal rite in the act of confession, where the person asks forgiveness of God, through the priest, by revealing their sins to the priest in the confessional, or at a penitential service where the priest asks the congregation to pray for their sins.

Funeral

A funeral service usually takes place within the first week after a Christian has died. Burial, or cremation, is the final part of the ceremony. The funeral service is always a solemn occasion, but is not melancholic as Christians believe that death is not the end of life, and they believe that all Christians

live on eternally in peace with God after their life on earth ends. Hope is
therefore the theme of a Christian funeral rite.

CHRISTIANITY

For further reading:

Hanson, A. & R.	REASONABLE BELIEF	O.U.P.
Johnson, P.	A HISTORY OF CHRISTIANITY	Penguin
Kung, H.	ON BEING A CHRISTIAN	Fount
Macquarrie, U.	TWENTIETH CENTURY RELIGIOUS THOUGHT	S.C.M.
Smart, N.	THE PHENOMENON OF CHRISTIANITY	Harper & Row
Ware, T.	THE ORTHODOX CHURCH	Penguin

ISLAM

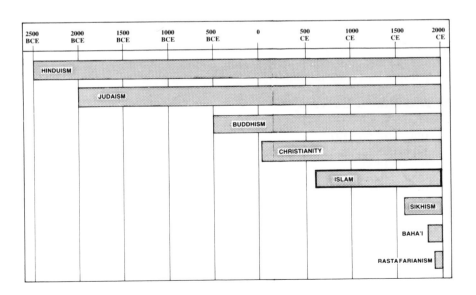

ISLAM

ORIGINS

Islam is an Arabic word which means 'submission', 'surrender' and 'obedience'. As a religion, Islam refers to the complete submission and obedience to *Allah*. (Allah is considered as the correct name of God as revealed in the *Qur'an* – believed by Muslims to be the final book of divine guidance.) The Islamic way of life is based on total obedience to Allah. This is the way to obtain peace and harmony: hence Islam also means peace.

A person who freely and consciously accepts the Islamic way of life and practices is called a *Muslim* – one who lives a life of submission and obedience. Islam is sometimes incorrectly called 'Muhammadanism' and the Muslims incorrectly called 'Muhammadans'. Though other religions, such as Christianity, are named after a person, Islam has not been named after the prophet *Muhammad* ('Peace Be Upon Him' is usually written following the naming of Muhammad). He is not believed to have founded the religion of Islam since it is accepted as the religion of all of God's messengers to mankind including Jesus. Muhammad closed the cycle of prophecy by restating, finally and clearly, the message of Allah.

BASIC BELIEFS

Islamic life is founded on both belief and action. These are considered both inseparable and complementary.

Seven Basic Beliefs

There are seven basic beliefs of Islam. These are concerned with:
1   one God (Allah)
2   his Angels
3   his Prophets
4   his Books
5   the Day of Judgement
6   predestination or Supremacy of Divine Will
7   life after Death.

These seven beliefs can be grouped into three:

> *Tawhid* – Oneness of Allah, Predestination or Supremacy of Divine Will.
>
> *Risalat* – Prophets of Allah, Books of Allah, Angels of Allah.
>
> *Akhirat* – The Day of Judgement, Life after Death.

Tawhid is the most important Islamic belief. It is a belief in one God, unique and without equal. Allah is creator, sustainer and nourisher of the entire universe. The unity and completeness of Allah is reflected throughout the universe.

Risalat has been the method of communicating guidance from Allah to humankind. Muslims believe that prophets and messengers have been sent to every nation at different times. They and the books of guidance they revealed, commanded humankind to follow the way of Allah. A Muslim accepts all of these revelations mentioned in the Qur'an (including the Psalms of David, the Torah of Moses, the Gospel of Jesus) though acknowledges the Qur'an as the final revelation.

Akhirat means life after death and is the ultimate reward for submission and obedience to Allah. Individuals become accountable for their actions on a Day of Judgement and are assigned a place in either Paradise or Hell. Conduct is as important in Islam as faith. The faith must lead to good action and morals in every aspect of life. Good deeds and morals are called *ibadah* which means worship. However, worship in Islam incorporates private and corporate devotion, benevolent social actions and human relationships.

Five Pillars of Islam

There are five basic duties which a Muslim must perform to provide the framework within which an entire life can be transformed into an act of worship. These five basic duties or pillars are:

1 Declaration of Faith (*Shahadah*)
2 Prayer, five times daily (*Salat*)
3 Welfare Contribution (*Zakat*)
4 Fasting during Ramadan (*Sawm*)
5 Pilgrimage to Mecca (*Hajj*)

Ash-Shahadah, the first of the five basic duties, is to pronounce knowingly and voluntarily the declaration of faith which is:

'There is no god except Allah, Muhammad is Allah's messenger.'

This declaration includes within it the central beliefs of *Tawhid* and *Risalat* explained earlier. It is regarded as the main pillar.

Salat is the second pillar of Islam and refers to compulsory prayers offered five times a day either individually or in congregation. The five daily prayers are:

Fajr	– dawn prayer
Zuhr	– after mid-day prayer
Asr	– late afternoon prayer
Maghrib	– after sunset prayer
Isha	– night prayer

Besides being a practical demonstration of faith Salat enables the Muslim to sustain constant contact with Allah and provides an opportunity to make adjustments and corrections to the pattern of life in order to maintain obedience to the will of Allah.

Zakat (welfare contribution) is the third pillar of Islam. It is a compulsory payment from the annual savings of a Muslim at the rate of 2½% on cash, jewellery and precious metals: there are other rates for the produce of agriculture. Zakat is not charity, which can be given in addition nor is it a tax which can be spent on anything. Zakat is an act of worship and the proceeds can only be used to help the less fortunate. Zakat helps to distribute wealth within an Islamic economy and remind Muslims that all wealth is Allah's and individuals are merely trustees of it.

Sawm (fasting in *Ramadan*) is the fourth pillar of Islam. All adult Muslims must fast from dawn to sunset every day during the ninth month of the Islamic calendar, Ramadan. Fasting means voluntarily abstaining from eating, drinking, smoking and sexual relations during the specified times. It is a deliberate programme of training in self-control and self-discipline leading to moral upgrading through refreshing a person's determination to fulfil their obligations to Allah.

Hajj is the fifth pillar of Islam. It is the pilgrimage to *Al-Kabah*, the House of Allah in Mecca, once in a lifetime by those Muslims who can afford the journey. Al-Kabah is a cube-shaped one storey building in Mecca and is believed to have been originally built by the *Prophet Adam* and later rebuilt by the *Prophet Ibrahim* (Abraham) and his son *Ismail* (Ishmael). The Hajj, which takes place in the twelfth month of the Islamic calendar *Dhu'l Hijjah*, becomes the opportunity for an annual gathering of the international Muslim congregation symbolising the unity of Muslims worldwide. Potential barriers of language, caste, race and nationalism disappear and people are united by the bond of faith.

IMPORTANT PEOPLE

Muhammad

Muhammad was born in *Mecca* (now in Saudi Arabia) on April 22nd 570 CE. His father *Abdullah*, a merchant, died before he was born and his mother *Amina* died when he was six. He was nurtured by his grandfather and after him by his uncle. As a young boy he travelled with his uncle on journeys in the merchant caravans and some years after that made similar journeys in the service of a successful businesswoman named *Khadija*. At the age of 25 he married Khadija.

In his late thirties or perhaps earlier he began to practise meditation and retreated for this purpose to a cave at Mount *Hira* on the outskirts of Mecca. It was there he received the 'call' and prophetic revelations through the Arch-Angel *Jibraeel* (Gabriel). The revelation accepted as the first states:

'Recite (or Read) in the name of God who created you. God created man with a clot of blood. Recite in the name of God who teaches by the pen. He teaches man those things which he does not know.' – Surah (chapter) 96 in the Qur'an.

The verb 'recite' produces the noun 'Qur'an' meaning 'reciting'.

Revelations continued over a period of years the main substance of which emphasised the Oneness of God, the Prophethood of Muhammad and Belief in an After Life. Further revelations occurred in Medina.

His preaching based upon the revelations in Mecca led to confrontation with the authorities in Mecca. He condemned idolatry and promoted mono-theism which clashed with the polytheistic tribal beliefs prevalent in Mecca. Though some were converted others persecuted him so that he and his fellow Muslims accepted an invitation to leave Mecca and go to the city of *Yathrib*, over 200 miles to the north of Mecca. This emigration or 'migra-tion' from Mecca is regarded as a significant event in Islamic and world history and marks the beginning of the Muslim calendar. The event is known as the *Hijrah*. The city of Yathrib became known as *Medinatal-Nabi* (Medina), or the 'city of the prophet'. The date of the Hijrah was 16th July, 622 CE.

In Medina Muhammad established a small Islamic community which had to defend itself against its opponents in Mecca. After eight years during which time two great battles were fought, Muhammad returned in triumph to Mecca. Meccans and many of the Arab tribes accepted Muhammad and Islam.

Muhammad died in 632 CE but Islam continued to expand under the leadership of the first *Caliph* (successor) *Abu Bakr* and his successors *Umar*, *Usman* and *Ali*. The rapid expansion of Islam remains one of the most significant events in world history.

To a Muslim, Muhammad provided the perfect example of obedience to Allah. During his life his followers recorded his sayings, actions and behaviour. These traditions of Muhammad are recorded in the *Hadith* and a Muslim needs to know the Hadith in order to understand and interpret the Qur'an. The *Sunnah* (right action as told by the prophet Mohammad) provides a Muslim with a human model. The divine model is the *Qur'an*.

IMPORTANT BOOKS

The Qur'an

The Qur'an is the heart of Islam. Muslims believe it to be the literal uncreated Word of God, inimitable and untranslatable revealed to Muham-mad over a period of years.

The Qur'an is divided into 114 chapters each called a *Surah* a word meaning 'eminence'. The surahs vary in length, the longest comprising one twelfth of the entire book. Each chapter is divided into sections each of which tends to cover one particular subject although the different sections are inter-related to each other. Each section is divided into verses and there are over 6,000 of these.

The Qur'an is treated with great reverence by Muslims. It is never placed beneath other books, nor on the ground and is placed on a stand when read. No one should eat or drink during its reading and silence must be observed during its narration. Muslims learn Arabic in order to read the Qur'an and some memorise it by heart and are able to add the title of *Hafiz* to their names as an honorary title. When not being read it is covered and placed on a high shelf.

The Qur'an deals with humankind and its ultimate goal in life. The teachings of the Qur'an address all areas of life, and life after death. They contain principles, doctrines and directions for all aspects of human life. It is a guide to salvation.

All events in the life of a Muslim involve reading passages from the Qur'an. Parts of it are recited in Muslim daily prayers and it is to be heard at the important rites of passage – birth, marriage and death.

It is inaccurate to regard the Qur'an as a life story of Muhammad. Though events relating to Muhammad and previous prophets are mentioned, the Qur'an is mainly about Allah and what people must do to lead a life pleasing to Allah. The theme of the Qur'an centres on the three fundamental ideas of *Tawhid*, *Risalat* and *Akhirat*. The eventual success of humankind on this earth and in the after-life is dependent on obedience to these central ideas (see 'Basic Beliefs').

IMPORTANT BUILDINGS

The Mosque

The word '*mosque*' is a corruption of the Arabic word '*masjid*' which means a place of prostration. A mosque is both a place of community prayer and a place of other community activities e.g. the *Madrassa* or Qur'an School. It has both sacred and secular functions which clearly reflects one of the main characteristics of the religion: that there should be no separation made between sacred and secular i.e. Muslims do not see their religious life as separate from family, business, social or political affairs.

Though mosques vary in shape and appearance most share some basic features. These are:

Sahn – an open courtyard where Muslims can study or talk.

Zulla – the carpeted prayer hall. The carpet, marked with parallel lines for the worshippers to align themselves on, is called the *sajjada*. Muslims often possess an individual sajjada decorated with scenes showing the interior of a mosque or *Al-kabah* embellished with Arabic calligraphy.

Qibla Wall – the wall facing the direction of Mecca and containing an alcove or niche called the *mihrab* towards which prayer is orientated.

Minaret – the tall tower from which the *muezzin* calls the faithful to prayer.

Minbar – this is a high, stepped platform from which a member of the congregation (possibly the *imam* or prayer leader) delivers the sermon at the Friday midday service.

Dikka – this is a platform usually supported on columns, found within larger mosques. Salat (prayer) is led from here and this enables all members of the congregation to perform prayer movements simultaneously. It is also the place from where the muezzin makes the second call to prayer immediately prior to its commencement.

In the mosque no images, statues or stained glass are allowed, nor any figurative representations. Two reasons are given for this prohibition:

Firstly, within Islam Allah is regarded as the sole Creator of a perfect universe and in a sense an artist is arrogantly attempting to re-create perfection;

Secondly, throughout the *Hadith* Muhammad condemns idolatry and emphasises *Tawhid* (the oneness of Allah).

In an idol, God is believed to exist and in many idols, many gods are thought to exist. Hence idols can lead to polytheistic beliefs and pose a threat to the fundamental doctrine of Tawhid. Decoration within the mosque is consequently based on Arabic calligraphy (usually extracts from the Qur'an) and arabesque patterns (complex geometric or abstract floral patterns).

IMPORTANT FESTIVALS

Islam has a number of special occasions of celebration. Participation is regarded as an act of devotion. The two major annual times of celebration are *Eid-ul-Fitr* and *Eid-ul-Adha*.

Eid-ul-Fitr is the Festival of Breaking the Fast of Ramadan. This is generally a national holiday in Muslim countries and when it occurs during term time in Britain Muslim parents may request a day off school for their children (as with Eid-ul-Adha). Muslims express their happiness by offering special congregational prayer, by tradition held in an open space, otherwise within the mosque. Some Muslim communities in Britain attempt to continue the tradition by gathering in park areas. Prior to the offer of *salat* (prayer) Muslims have to pay *Zakat-ul-Fitr* (almsgiving). Following prayers it is customary for Muslims to tend the graves of dead relatives and on their return home a special meal is eaten and family visits take place. Eid greeting cards and gifts are exchanged and new clothes worn.

Eid-ul-Adha is the Festival of Sacrifice and takes place in the twelfth month of the Islamic year and at the end of the season for completing of Hajj (pilgrimage). Participants in the Hajj commemorate the occasion when Ibrahim (Abraham) was prepared to sacrifice his own son, Ismail (Ishmael). Non-participants in the Hajj are able to share the experience of the Hajji (a participant in the Hajj) through this festival. It takes the same form as Eid-ul-Fitr only without the zakat (almsgiving). Following the offering of special prayers, families sacrifice a sheep, goat or cow, according to their means.

The meat is distributed amongst neighbours and the poor. Some is retained for a special festival meal. Greeting cards and visits are once again exchanged.

Other occasions of celebration include:

Lailat-ul-Qadr (The Night of Power) celebrated during Ramadan and commemorating the first revelation of the Qur'an to Muhammad. The Qur'an is read through during the last few days of Ramadan and additional prayers are offered.

Lailat-ul-Bar'h (The Night of Forgiveness) celebrated before Ramadan and an occasion to forgive prolonged grievances and arguments with others.

Al-Hijrah (New Year's Day) commemorates the Hijrah or migration of Muhammad from Mecca to Medina in 622 CE which led to establishment of the Muslim community. Gifts are exchanged and stories are told of Muhammad and his companions.

Mulad-ul-Nabi (The Birthday of the Prophet Muhammad). Stories and lectures on the life of Muhammad are presented in the mosque.

Islamic festivals are celebrated according to the Islamic calendar which is based on lunar months and is roughly 11 days shorter than the Gregorian calendar based on solar months. This means that the Islamic calendar moves 'backwards' each year so that Muslim festivals fall at different times each year in relation to the Gregorian calendar. Over a period of time particular Muslim festivals will be celebrated during different British seasons. Festival dates are determined by the sighting of the new moon with the naked eye. Dates according to the Islamic calendar are termed AH – *'After the Hijrah'*.

IMPORTANT RELIGIOUS PRACTICES

Muslim Worship
Friday, particularly for mid-day prayers, is the important day of assembly for Muslims. Muslims are summoned to worship by a call to prayer, the *adhan* or *azzan*. This is delivered by the muezzin from the minaret in Muslim countries but often from within the mosque in Britain. The adhan is delivered in Arabic and consists of seven lines which are repeated several times and incorporate *Ash Shahadah*, the basic creed of Islam.

The Adhan
Allah is most great (repeated 4 times)
I bear witness that there is no god but Allah (twice)
I bear witness that Muhammad is the Prophet of Allah (twice)
Come to Prayer (twice)

Come to Salvation (twice)
Allah is most Great (twice)
There is no God but Allah (once).

Prior to the commencement of salat (the obligatory ritual prayer) a second call to prayer is delivered. This resembles the adhan but includes the line, 'Prayer is ready' following the line 'Come to Salvation'.

Before the performance of salat Muslims ritually wash themselves. This is called *wudu* or *wuzu* and is completed in the ablutions area of the mosque before each set time for prayer. Wudu consists of a precisely defined procedure for washing the face, mouth, nostrils, hands and forearms, the whole head and behind the ears and the feet. Each part is washed three times. Once physically clean the worshipper proceeds to attain inner cleansing of the spirit through salat.

Though a Muslim can offer personal prayer, salat follows a precise pattern of body movements related to set Arabic words. Before entering the prayer hall shoes are removed, men cover their heads as a sign of submission to Allah and women dress modestly, ensuring that only the face and hands are exposed. In fact women do not attend the mosque as often as men and when they do they usually worship in a different room though in a similar manner. This involves a series of movements involving standing, bowing, prostrating and sitting accompanied by spoken words. Cumulatively the movements and words are called a *rak'a* (see illustrations). A particular

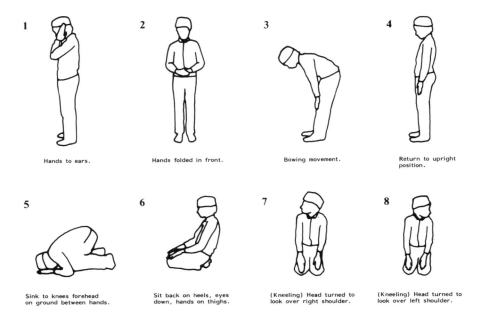

1   Hands to ears.

2   Hands folded in front.

3   Bowing movement.

4   Return to upright position.

5   Sink to knees forehead on ground between hands.

6   Sit back on heels, eyes down, hands on thighs.

7   (Kneeling) Head turned to look over right shoulder.

8   (Kneeling) Head turned to look over left shoulder.

number of these must be offered at each set prayer time. Following the offering of the final rak'a the worshipper maintains the sitting position and performs the last action, the *salam*. The worshipper turns his or her head to the right and says 'Peace be with you and the Mercy of Allah' to fellow Muslims and the angels and then repeats the words with the head turned to the left.

The essence of Islam – submission to Allah – is clearly emphasised in the prostration and the utterance of the *takbir*: 'Allah is Most Great'. Islam means 'to submit' but also means 'peace and harmony'. Through submission spiritual peace and harmony may be achieved provided the external ritual is matched by an inner conviction.

Food and Drink

There are regulations regarding diet which must be observed by all Muslims. Within Islam, lawful food is known as *halal* and forbidden food as *haram*. Muslims are forbidden to eat:

Dead animals and birds

Animals slain without the invocation of the name of Allah

Animals strangled to death

Pig meat

Carnivorous animals

Animals devoured by wild beasts

The blood of animals

Muslims may eat all kinds of fruit and vegetables as well as fish. However, there is stringent discrimination with regard to meats. Pig and carnivorous animals are forbidden. This includes foodstuffs made from meat products such as corned beef and soups, and foods containing lard such as bread and ice-cream.

Halal meat is slaughtered according to Islamic law. This method involves a sharp knife severing the inner part of the animal's neck to allow the maximum drainage of blood. During this ritual slaughtering the name of Allah is invoked i.e. 'In the name of Allah, the Compassionate, the Merciful'.

Islam forbids the consumption of alcohol in any form. This includes its use in cooking and for medical purposes, unless there is positively no other substitute. Tradition suggests that Muhammad, when asked about alcohol as a medicine, said 'It is not medicine, it is a disease'. A Muslim should not really offer alcohol to a non-Muslim guest, nor permit its sale if he owns a shop or restaurant.

Muslims believe that alcohol not only leads to addiction and waste but also affects a person's ability to perform religious duties within the family and wider community. It damages self-control and the ability to relate to Allah through prayer.

Dress

Islam specifies that modesty and simplicity should govern choice of dress. For men this means that their bodies must be covered from the navel to the knees, and for women, the whole body except the face, hands and feet. Dress expressing arrogance should not be chosen and the style largely depends on local custom and climatic conditions.

Marriage and Family Life

Marriage is considered to be the basis of family life in Islam. Muslim marriages are generally arranged by parents with the consent of the boy and girl. Marriage is a civil contract in Islam but it is viewed as a mutual agreement made between the man and the woman before Allah and humankind. The ceremony can be as simple or as ornate as one wishes and can take place at any convenient place. A knowledgeable Muslim, usually the Imam, officiates. Appropriate passages from the Qur'an are read and an address on the religious significance of marriage and on the responsibilities and rights of the husband and wife is given. At this stage marriage vows are made and a written contract signed. Muslim law demands that the man should give his wife a marriage gift (the *mehr* or dowry). This is usually a sum of money which remains the property of the wife.

It is permissible for a man to have up to four wives, but, as they must all be supported equally, on economic grounds alone, it is usually the practice to have only one wife. Monogamy also helps to overcome the complicated problem of legal difficulties and definitions in non-Islamic countries where only one wife is recognised in law.

Within the family husband and wife are considered to be equal partners though each has role obligations and rights which are clearly defined within the Qur'an. The husband's main responsibility is acknowledged to be that of wage provider and head of the family. The wife's main responsibility is concerned with the domestic organisation of the family. This role is seen as vital and has parity with that of the husband since a great deal of status and power is given to the wife because of the prime importance of family life within Muslim communities. Islamic teaching values marriage and attempts to promote family stability by regarding divorce, which can be initiated by the husband, as the most abominable of permitted acts.

Birth

The birth of a child is a time of great rejoicing for a Muslim family as it is for any other family. Each child is regarded as a gift from Allah and the parents have a responsibility to Allah and to society for the nurturing of the infant. The Muslim regards certain days as being particularly significant.

On the day of the birth, the *adhan* (call to prayer) is recited into the infant's right ear, with the added words 'We are standing up for prayer' into the left.

A week after the birth, the family and their friends gather for the naming ceremony. The baby is named by the father following the recitation of passages from the Qur'an. Male infants are circumcised and the head is shaved in order to symbolically rid the child of all misfortune. The child's hair is weighed and the equivalent weight of gold and silver is given to charity.

At the age of four years, four months and four days the child is taught the first words of the Qur'an. This is known as the *Bismillah* ceremony and marks the beginning of the child's religious training.

Death

In the Muslim faith there are a number of rites that take place at the time of a person's death. A Muslim close to death will recite the *Shahada*, the basic statement of faith. At death, family and friends gather in the home to express their sorrow, recite the Qur'an and pray for Allah's mercy and forgiveness. Burial takes place 'without delay' according to the teaching of Muhammad.

Prior to the burial it is customary for the body to be washed by members of the same sex and shrouded in clean white sheets – often the garments worn by the dead person when on the pilgrimage to Mecca. The corpse is placed in a coffin which is taken to the mosque where special funeral prayers are offered. The body is buried with the face lying in the direction of Mecca. Muslims are not cremated. The period of mourning continues for not more than seven days and on the seventh day friends and relatives will offer prayers at the graveside.

Muslims believe that death is a doorway to another existence. The dead are said to be met at the grave by angels who assess the individual's belief in Allah and the Prophets. Believers exist in peace and happiness until the Day of Judgement whilst unbelievers experience punishment and discomfort. At the end of time, on the Day of Judgement, all who have died will be physically resurrected – hence burial rather than cremation. Those who have been faithful to the guidance of Allah will exist in Paradise. Those who have rejected Allah will be separated from him in Hell. The Qur'an vividly describes these two opposite states.

According to Islamic beliefs therefore, each individual is responsible for his or her ultimate destiny. If one is a true believer and seeks forgiveness for misdeeds, the Muslim is confident that Allah will be merciful.

ISLAM

For further reading:

Ahmad, K.	ISLAM: ITS MEANING AND MESSAGE	Islamic Council of Europe
Bell, R.	INTRODUCTION TO THE QUR'AN	Edinburgh Univ. Press
Guillaume, A.	ISLAM	Penguin
Nasr, S. H.	IDEALS AND REALITIES OF ISLAM	Allen & Unwin
Man's Religious Quest (AD 208)	ISLAM AND THE MUSLIM	Open University
Tames, R.	APPROACHES TO ISLAM	John Murray.

SIKHISM

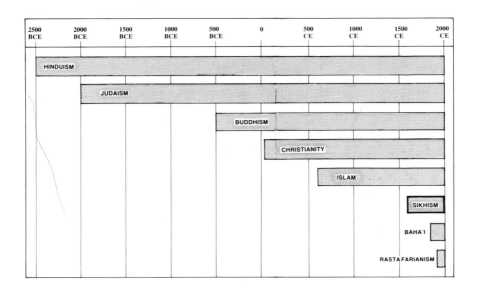

SIKHISM

ORIGINS

The Sikh religion originated in the area of Pakistan and north-west India called the Punjab. The name Punjab originated from two Persian words 'panj' (five) and 'ab' (water) and therefore the Punjab is termed the 'land of the five rivers'. It is an area bounded in the north by the foothills of the Himalayas from which the five rivers, each a tributary of the River Indus, flow. Since 1947 the Indian state of Punjab has been approximately one third of the size of the original geographical region. The vast majority of the world's twelve million Sikhs live in the Indian state of Punjab though some have formed sizeable minorities in other states and the larger Indian cities. About two million have migrated from the Indian sub-continent and have established communities in Canada, the United States, East Africa, New Zealand, Australia and Britain. Britain has the largest Sikh population outside India.

Within orthodox Sikhism the faith originated with a direct revelation from God to a chosen disciple, *Guru Nanak*, during the late 15th and early 16th centuries. Through this revelation Guru Nanak assimilated a facet of the divine and creative word which was passed on unaltered through his teaching to a series of nine historical figures each of whom was called Guru. After about two hundred years the divine word became invested within the sacred scriptures (*Guru Granth Sahib*) and the community of disciples (*Guru Panth*).

However, Sikhism is also seen by some scholars to reflect elements of the social, political and religious environment within which it originated and acquired its most distinctive features, though scholars differ in their view of the extent and significance of these influences. Some forward an eclectic interpretation of the origins of the religion pointing to the way Sikhism appears to combine elements of Hinduism and Islam. Others point to the similarities between the doctrines taught by Guru Nanak and those of his contemporaries and other antecedent philosophies, though they acknowledge that Guru Nanak did not simply mediate the ideas of others but transformed them into a coherent school of thought. Guru Nanak's personal experiences from the perspective of his own social background and the history of India during the 16th and 17th centuries are also put forward as important influences on the nature of Sikhism.

BASIC BELIEFS

God

The opening words of the Sikh scriptures (the *Guru Granth Sahib*) are known as the *Mool Mantra* and convey the central belief about God. This Mool Mantra (literally 'basic' or 'perfect' incantation) begins with the symbolic utterance '*Ik Oankar*' (There is one God). The symbol representing this statement of faith, like the mystic symbol '*OM*' within Hinduism, stands for the unity that is Absolute and Eternal Reality. In this transcendent state God is essentially indescribable, being without form and without qualities.

However, God (Parmeshur) offers humankind salvation by graciously revealing aspects of himself through all creation. The remainder of the Mool Mantra begins the revelation of the divine attributes: Eternal Truth, Creator, Without Fear, Without Hatred, Timeless, Formless, Beyond Birth and Death, Self-Enlightened. God is personal in the sense that he is present in all creation, evident to those who diligently seek him but constant within those yet to apprehend his presence. God is not personal in the anthropomorphic sense associated with the divine manifestations (avatars) within the Hindu tradition.

Man (Humankind)

Humankind is unique within God's creation in that it possesses the capacity to seek out the divine revelation within creation and consequently responds to it by acknowledging dependence upon it. However, too often humankind's ignorance dominates. Man begins to see himself as self-reliant (*haumai*) and tends to follow the guidance of his own mind, becoming worldly-conscious (*manmukh*). This creates an illusory duality where humankind and the temporal world are thought to be distinct from the Eternal God. This state of being is termed *maya* and denotes anything that prevents concentration on the search for the Truth and union with God.

Within Sikhism maya is over-attachment to worldly values. Sikhism believes in the reality of the divinely created universe not regarding it as ultimately illusory as in the Hindu concept of maya. Within Sikhism it is worldly values that are a delusion.

The result of this materialistic perspective on reality and the consequent alienation from God is that humankind becomes subject to the law of *karma* i.e. the principle that certain actions reap certain reactions, good or bad, according to how those activities benefit or harm others. The operation of the law of karma is associated with transmigration. Within Sikhism, God desires the salvation of humankind from this and yet permits the principle of karma to operate. This is indicative of the relative autonomy humankind possesses within God's creation. Salvation may be attained when humankind appreciates that this must be dependent and not independent autonomy. This occurs when humankind becomes *gurmukh* (God-conscious or God-filled).

Salvation (Mukti)

Salvation consists of escape from *haumai* (self-centredness) and complete perception of the *hukam* (the divinely inspired order and unity of all existence). Salvation is to become part of this divine order rather than detached from it. This can only be attained through an awareness of the inner presence of God acquired through concentration on the word of God (*Sabda*) or the name of God (*Nam*). Eager that humankind should experience salvation, God graciously manifests himself in these forms.

Humankind must meditate upon the Name of God (Nam), a term encompassing the very nature and being of God and not merely a symbol. This meditation may be *nam japana* – a mechanical repetition of a chosen name of God such as '*Waheguru*' meaning 'Wonderful Lord'. More often it is termed *nam simaran* which refers to the human personality being gradually altered through action undertaken with the Name of God perpetually in mind. With God's grace this makes salvation attainable within the context of a single ordinary, everyday life, though generally it is acknowledged that it is attained in stages that may span more than one existence. The steps to this state of mystical bliss are viewed as regions (*Khands*) of perfection and are set out by Guru Nanak in four hymns found in the Guru Granth Sahib.

The emphasis within Sikh religious thought on the individual's requirement to become aware of God within themselves and to do so in the context of everyday life within this world, God's creation, has given Sikhism particular ethical and social ideals. Living a life of service in the world is as great a virtue as participation in ceremonies and rituals. Guru Nanak regarded rituals and ceremonies as potentially 'chains of the mind'. Asceticism is rejected in favour of God-orientated worldliness. Guru Nanak said 'Not the ascetic way, but a life of truth and love amid the world's temptations, is the secret of spiritual life'. Since God pervades every heart, differentiation on the basis of caste, class, race and sex is rejected on both theological and social grounds. Many of the important religious practices within Sikhism illustrate some of these ideals and the virtues that extend from them.

IMPORTANT PEOPLE

Within Sikhism the faith is believed to have been revealed through a series of messengers called *Gurus*. Though each of the ten Sikh Gurus contributed to the development of Sikhism each is believed to have shared the same religious truth and to have possessed the same unique insight into God. Regarded as human rather than divine, the Sikh Gurus are revered but not worshipped. They are considered to be individuals enlightened by God and hence freed from the cycle of rebirth but commissioned by God to lead others to liberation. Although the Sikhs give precedence to their own Gurus, they also acknowledge such individuals as the Buddha, Moses, Jesus and Muhammad as messengers of God, though they would not accept the notion of incarnation as expressed within Christianity and Hinduism.

Guru Nanak (1469–1539)

The first Guru has become a focus of devotion to a greater extent than any of his successors. Guru Nanak is known through the many hymns which he wrote and perhaps less certainly through the hagiographic narratives compiled fifty or more years after his death.

He was born in a village called Talwandi near Lahore, the largest city in the Punjab region in North India. Now Talwandi is called Nankana Sahib and is within Pakistan. He was a Hindu by birth, a member of the Kshatriya caste, which entitled him to study the ancient Sanskrit scriptures, the Vedas. The area in which he was born was under Muslim rule and as a young man Nanak was employed by a Muslim official. Although he was therefore familiar with two religious traditions, neither appeared to provide a satisfactory focus for his own personal religious growth.

Passages in the Guru Granth Sahib, the Sikh Holy Scriptures, relate an apparently transforming experience that occurred in Nanak's life around the age of 30. While performing ritual ablutions he is said to have been taken to the court of God where he consumed a cup of nectar (*amrit*) with the command 'This is the cup of the adoration of God's name. Drink it. I am with you. I bless you and raise you up. Whoever remembers you will enjoy my favour. Go, rejoice in my name and teach others to do so. I have bestowed the gift of my name upon you. Let this be your calling.' It is accepted that Nanak's first poetic declaration following this religious experience was *The Mool Mantra* which enshrines the concept of the Divinity he had encountered.

The story is a statement that Nanak's experience was inspired by God and therefore he was not merely a self-appointed teacher. For the next twenty-two years he embarked on a number of missionary journeys in order to reveal the message of God's Name to the world. The latter part of his life was spent within a community founded at Kartarpur.

According to Hindu tradition a guru should be a member of the Brahmin or priestly caste and should teach the Vedas in Sanskrit and only to members of the first three or twice-born castes (Brahmins, Kshatriyas and Vaishyas). During this foundation period of Sikhism, Guru Nank proclaimed a directly inspired message rather than one based on Vedic revelations. He also taught members of all castes including the lowest (Shudras)

71

and in native dialect rather than Sanskrit. His message was therefore accessible to many more people and appealed to those for whom Hinduism offered little hope and Islam an unacceptable alternative.

At some time in his ministry at Kartarpur, Guru Nanak nominated a man called Lehna to be his successor and nurtured him to become the leader of the community. This man's name was changed to Angad, which means 'my limb' and emphasises the Sikh view that each Guru was faithful to the same message received and taught by Guru Nanak.

Guru Angad (1504–1552)

Guru Angad began gathering together the hymns of Guru Nanak that were to form the basis of the Guru Granth Sahib, the Sikh Holy Book, and his role as a consolidator in the early years of the Sikh community (Panth) is viewed as extremely important. He initiated the building of early Sikh temples which were used both for worship and educating the community. Some traditions accredit the invention of the *gurmukhi* script, a form of Punjabi in which the Guru Granth Sahib is written, to Guru Angad and some also say that it was his encouragement that led to the completion of the *janam sakhi*, the biography of Guru Nanak.

Guru Amar Das (1479–1574)

The development of the central importance of the *langar* (communal kitchen) is ascribed to Guru Amar Das. The *Guru Ka Langar* enabled the emphasis on the unity and equality of mankind contained within Guru Nanak's message to be promoted. Distinctions on the basis of caste, sex or religion are not permitted during this common meal. The third Guru also assembled the Sikhs at his base at Goindwal three times a year at the time of the Hindu festivals. This action challenged his followers to show that they had abandoned Hindu rituals in favour of the new teaching.

Guru Ram Das (1534–1581)

Guru Ram Das is mainly remembered as the founder of the city of Amritsar on land apparently donated by the Mogul Emperor, Akbar, regarded by the Sikhs as a tolerant Muslim ruler. One of the hymns composed by Guru Ram Das is an important feature of the Sikh wedding ceremony.

Guru Arjan (1563–1606)

Under Guru Arjan's leadership Amritsar was completed and other towns were constructed. In 1589 the building of the Harmandir at Amritsar was started and soon completed. The present day Golden Temple, built in the nineteenth century, stands on this site. Guru Arjan also produced an authoritative collection of Sikh scriptures called the *Adi Granth* ('adi' – first, 'granth' – collection) which were installed in the *Harmandir* (the Lord's House) in Amritsar in 1604. On the death of the Mogul Emperor, Akbar, the relationship between Sikhs and Muslims deteriorated and eventually Guru Arjan was arrested. He was tortured to death and is revered as the first martyr-Guru of the Sikhs.

Guru Hargobind (1595–1644)

With the accession of Hargobind to the Guru-ship there was a noticeable change of emphasis in leadership. The Sikhs began to arm themselves for protection against Mogul oppression and the ideal of Sikhs as 'saint-soldiers' emerged. It was during the time of Guru Hargobind that the symbolic pennant (the *Nishan Sahib*) which is flown outside the place of worship, was instituted. The symbol is of two swords: one representing temporal power and one spiritual authority.

Guru Har Rai (1630–1661)

This period of Sikh history was marked by an attempt to revert to the tolerant relationship between Sikh and Muslim that had existed during the time of Guru Arjan. Guru Har Rai had little success however and before he died he nominated his young son aged five to follow him as Guru.

Guru Har Krishan (1656–1664)

Guru Har Krishan's leadership was unacceptable to the Mogul rulers who imprisoned him at Delhi where he died three years later after contracting smallpox.

Guru Tegh Bahadur (1621–1675)

The ninth Guru was the youngest son of Guru Hargobind who had twice been passed over in earlier years. He displayed the qualities needed at a time of increasing persecution and Islamisation by the Mogul rulers. Guru Tegh Bahadur was respected for his piety and commitment to thwarting the religious intolerance of his day. He was eventually imprisoned and was executed at Delhi when he refused to convert to Islam. A magnificent Gurdwara (Sikh place of worship) was erected at the site of the death of the second martyr-Guru of the Sikhs.

Guru Gobind Singh (1666–1708)

Guru Gobind Singh is seen as the most important Guru after Guru Nanak as a consequence of two particular events. The first occurred in 1699 and marked the transference of the authority of the individual living Guru to the Sikh religious community as a whole. Sikh tradition describes how the *Panth* (literally 'path' – a term used to describe the community seeking religious truth) was formally established by Guru Gobind Singh at Anandpur. Conscious of the need to strengthen and unify the Sikhs Guru Gobind Singh addressed his followers, gathered together in Anandpur at his request, concerning the prime importance of obedience, courage and loyalty. The nature of the address was very tense and dramatic.

Guru Gobind Singh introduced a rite of initiation into the Sikh faith during which Sikh men and women were compelled to express allegiance to the community (Guru Panth) and not merely to an individual Guru. Initiated members of this new community of 'Pure Ones' – *the Khalsa* – adopted a uniform and the common surname *Kaur* and *Singh*, which mean 'princess' and 'lion' respectively. This was to create equality, since surnames signified a particular caste. Through this act Guru Gobind Singh created a group of people mutually responsible for the faith no longer reliant on charismatic individual leaders.

In 1708 Gobind Singh altered the nature of guruship further. Before he died of wounds sustained at the hands of an assassin, Guru Gobind Singh announced that he would have no human successor. Instead he installed the scripture, compiled earlier by Guru Arjan and later revised, as Guru. He affirmed that this book was the final and everlasting Guru and should be called 'Guru Granth Sahib' meaning 'Holy Book which is Lord'.

Spiritual and temporal guidance now resided within the Guru Panth and the Guru Granth Sahib, and Sikhism was firmly established as a permanent and separate religion.

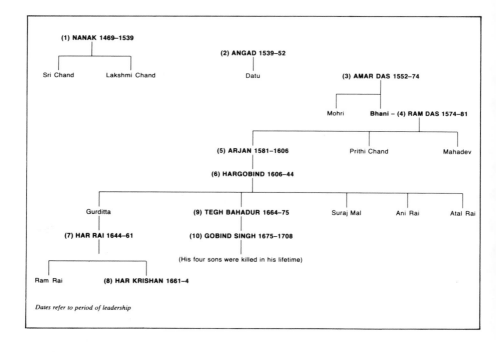

IMPORTANT BOOKS

There are two important books of sacred writings within Sikhism. The first is the *Adi Granth* ('first collection') which is believed to contain the word of divine truth expressed through the hymns of six of the Sikh Gurus. This scripture also contains the writings of other Sikhs such as Murdana, a companion of Guru Nanak, and of twelve non-Sikhs from various religious backgrounds. The inclusion of these works emphasises the open and universal nature of Sikhism.

The second scripture is called the *Dasam Granth* ('collection of the tenth Guru') and contains the writings of Guru Gobind Singh compiled after his death by one of his disciples.

The first version of the Adi Granth was produced during the time of Guru Angad, the second Guru, but it was Guru Arjan who compiled an authoritative collection and the original copy dating from 1604 is preserved in the Harmandir in Amritsar. The tenth Guru Gobind Singh finalised the collection though he did not include any of his own writings within it. He declared the scripture to be the final and immortal Guru and its new title, *Guru Granth Sahib* reflected its enhanced status.

The Guru Granth Sahib is not structured into books, chapters and verses and does not contain narrative passages. It is made up of poetic hymns in praise of God and exhortations to listen to God's voice within one's heart. The hymns are arranged into 31 divisions each one set to a different Indian musical form or *raga*, to which it should be sung, with the exception of the Japji which is used in meditation and is spoken. The *Japji*, compiled by Guru Nanak and located at the beginning of the Guru Granth Sahib, incorporates the *Mool Mantra* and centres on the theme of the nature of God.

Each copy of the Guru Granth Sahib is an exact reproduction of the edition compiled by Guru Gobind Singh. Every copy contains 5,894 hymns written on 1,430 pages. Thus, for example, the wedding hymn written by Guru Ram Das called the *Lavan* will always be found on page 773 or AG (773).

The status of the Guru Granth Sahib within Sikhism means that it is accorded great reverence and respect. This is shown in its central location in the place of worship as well as in its use in services and other facets of Sikh life.

IMPORTANT BUILDINGS

A Sikh *Gurdwara* (which means 'the Guru's door') is principally a place where the Guru Granth Sahib is located and where the congregation of Sikhs may gather around it. The building may be of any size or shape and although purpose-built temples have been constructed in Britain, houses and former churches have been converted. One distinguishing external feature is the *Nishan Sahib*, the Sikh flag, comprising a double-edged sword (*khanda*), two curved swords (*kirpans*), and a circle (*chakra*) on a saffron coloured triangular-shaped cloth attached to a pole. The insignia on the flag is usually called the *Khanda*, derived from the central symbol.

The *Khanda* is the insignia of the Sikhs. It is composed of three symbols though its name is derived from the central symbol. The *Khanda*, double-edged sword, symbolises the One God; the *Chakkar*, circle, God's infiniteness; and the two *Kirpans* spiritual power (peeri) and temporal power (meeri).

Internally the main room in the building is dominated by the Guru Granth Sahib. The holy book is placed on a stool (*manji*) which itself is on a platform or dais called the *takht*, which means 'throne', covered with fine material. Above the book is a silk canopy. The whole is enclosed within a beautiful structure called the *palki*. When not being read the Granth itself will be covered with a cloth called a *romalla* or removed ceremonially to a separate room.

The takht stands free from the walls of the building so that circumambulation of the holy book can take place during particular ceremonies. In front of the takht there may be another cloth upon which offerings are placed and musicians (*ragis*) will be seated to the side during services. The congregation sits on a carpeted floor facing the Granth upon its throne. This arrangement is a constant reminder of the status of the scriptures and also emphasises the equality within the congregation. Pictures of the Gurus may adorn the walls of the building.

The *Langar* (meaning 'free kitchen') is another essential feature of a Gurdwara. All worshippers, Sikh and non-Sikh alike, gather in a room to participate in a communal meal after the service, symbolising once again the egalitarian ideals within Sikhism.

In Britain the Gurdwara is an important social and religious centre for the Sikh community. In addition to its role in worship the Gurdwara plays an important part in the education of Sikh children assuring the transmission of essential aspects of Sikh culture to the young.

IMPORTANT FESTIVALS

Sikh festivals are related to the Hindu lunar calendar and are consequently variable. An exception is the celebration of the new religious year within Sikhism which has been fixed on April 13th each year (*Baisakhi* or *Vaisakhi*).

There are two types of festival within Sikhism, *melas* which are meetings or fairs and *gurpurbs* which are holidays linked with either the births or deaths of particular Gurus.

Melas correspond to Hindu festivals but in order to emphasise the separateness of Sikhism they have been given a new significance. Since the time of Guru Amar Das it has been traditional for Sikhs to assemble together at certain times in the Hindu festival calendar. Three particular occasions remain important:

Baisakhi – Originally a time to propitiate the Hindu gods prior to the harvest, it became a period of instruction in the teachings of the Sikh Gurus. With the passage of time it became an occasion to celebrate the founding of the Sikh *Khalsa* by Guru Gobind Singh at Anandpur in 1699.

The first five members of this brotherhood were selected by Gobind after they had offered to sacrifice their lives for their Guru. Apparently executed they were then dramatically presented to the assembled gathering emphasising the need to be prepared to offer the ultimate sacrifice in defence of the faith. The *Panj Pyares*, the 'Beloved Five' were initiated by drinking a symbolic nectar and many of the Sikhs present were similarly baptised into the Khalsa. They adopted a common title and a uniform commonly termed the Five Ks (*Panj Kakke*).

Today Baisakhi is viewed as the birthday of modern Sikhism and is a time when new members are often initiated and elections for the Gurdwara committees are held. In the Punjab, Baisakhi is very much a fair at which farmers buy and sell all kinds of agricultural produce.

Diwali – Within Hinduism this is a festival of light, celebrating the victory of good over evil. To Sikhs it commemorates the release of Guru Hargobind, the sixth Guru, from captivity at the hands of the Mogul Emperor Jehangir and the way in which he benevolently negotiated the release of fifty-two Hindu princes who were imprisoned with him. To Sikhs, Diwali is an occasion to celebrate the importance of freedom and lights are lit in Sikh homes as they were lit around the Golden Temple at Amritsar following Hargobind's triumphal return. Today the Golden Temple is still illuminated and firework displays are arranged. It is now deemed appropriate to exchange presents and greetings cards too.

Hola Mohalla – Holi for Hindus is a Krishan festival marking the beginning of Spring and is characterised by carefree rejoicing particularly popular with ordinary people. In order to discourage Sikhs from being tempted into the festivities, Guru Gobind Singh instituted Hola Mahalla in 1680. During this assembly of the Sikhs military manoeuvres, displays and processions were organised. It is still common for athletic competitions to be held though with an emphasis on fun.

Gurpurbs are holidays associated with particular gurus. In India these occasions may involve processions at the head of which a copy of the Guru Granth Sahib, guarded by five armed Sikhs, rests. Hymns are sung and formal addresses given concerning the attributes of the Guru who is being commemorated.

In Britain a special weekend service (*diwan*) is held and there is a complete continuous reading of the holy book (*Akhand Path*). During the forty-eight hours this takes place Sikhs will attempt to attend the Gurdwara for some time each day but particularly when the ceremonial reading is being concluded prior to the Sunday worship. When worship is over, all attend the Langar, the communal meal.

Four festivals particularly important to the international Sikh community are:

the birthday of Guru Nanak
the birthday of Guru Gobind Singh
the martyrdom of Guru Arjun
the martyrdom of Guru Tegh Bahadur.

IMPORTANT RELIGIOUS PRACTICES

Worship

Sikhs have no mandatory holy day designated for worship and there is often a gathering of members of a local Sikh community on weekday mornings and evenings, although there are no fixed times for worship during the day either. Sunday has been adopted as a regular day for worship by those Sikhs living in Britain, to blend in with the Christian holy day.

There are no ordained priests within Sikhism though worship may be led by a *Granthi*, a knowledgeable and respected member of the community. He and others may take on certain official responsibilities within the Gurdwara.

Before entering into the presence of God – as entry into the room where the Guru Granth is installed is viewed – a Sikh will bathe, remove shoes and cover the head. Tobacco and other intoxicants must not be taken into the precincts of the Gurdwara.

On entry the worshipper should approach the Guru Granth Sahib, bow, and kneel down placing the forehead on the floor momentarily. This respectful ritual is preceded by the presentation of an offering which may take the form of money, food or a cloth (*romalla*) which will be used to cover the holy scriptures. Worshippers then seat themselves on the floor facing the Granth.

The act of corporate worship (diwan) which then follows does not conform to a prescribed liturgy though the latter stages of the service and other Sikh ceremonies follow a common pattern. The diwan may last a number of hours with worshippers entering at different times. Such a service may include someone intoning randomly chosen extracts from the Guru Granth Sahib and the singing of devotional hymns (*kirtan*) to the accompaniment of musicians. Hymns may be interspersed with lectures or sermons. Whenever the holy scriptures are open a fan made from peacocks feathers or yak hair (*chauri*) is waved over the exposed pages. The chauri is a symbol of the regal authority of the Granth over the Sikh community. Two religious acts conclude the diwan and every Sikh ceremony: these are the saying of the *Ardas* prayer and the distribution of *Karah Parshad*.

While the congregation is standing an individual will offer the *Ardas* prayer on behalf of the community who join in at the end of each section of the prayer by saying 'Waheguru' (Wonderful Lord). Personal prayers may be offered at this time and finally a verse chosen at random from the Granth is read as a parting thought and guidance.

Karah Parshad, a sacred sweet food is served to all those present. This is not a sacrament but another demonstration of the egalitarian nature of Sikhism. The *Langar* or communal meal which may also follow diwan has the same intent as Karah Parshad.

Private devotion is also an integral part of Sikh worship. Since Sikhism teaches that God is within each human being, individuals have the responsibility to seek for God within themselves. The practice of meditation, perhaps using prayer beads (*mala*), and the recitation of the *Japji*, a hymn composed by Guru Nanak, or the Jap (a poem written by Guru Gobind Singh) are important aspects of this personal quest. Opportunities for private meditation also exist within diwan.

Pilgrimage

Pilgrimage is not obligatory within Sikhism and the Sikh Gurus expressed scepticism concerning its practice within Hinduism and Islam. When challenged over the place of pilgrimage in the human religious quest, Guru Nanak said 'God's Name is the real pilgrimage place which consists of the Word of God, and the cultivation of inner knowledge' (AG 687). However, the Golden Temple in Amritsar is a place many Sikhs desire to visit and the personal motivation for this is obviously varied.

Food

Quite a number of Sikhs are vegetarians although the faith is not clearly prescriptive on this matter. Gurdwaras do not serve meat in the Langar. One particular obligation placed upon members of the Khalsa is to avoid meat slaughtered according to Muslim practice.

Initiated Sikhs should also avoid tobacco narcotics and other intoxicants, including alcohol. These injunctions extend to the trading in these commodities too.

Dress

The *turban* has become synonymous with Sikhism although it is worn by people of other religions within the Indo-Pakistan sub-continent. From the earliest days the turban became an aspect of religious and social identity to the Sikhs, encouraging a sense of belonging to a separate religious tradition. Whilst participating in sports events, Sikhs may replace the turban with a small scarf called a *patka* which is knotted at the top to keep the hair intact. Guru Nanak himself began the tradition of keeping hair intact and covering the head with a turban and this was continued by the other Gurus. Guru Arjan encouraged men to maintain their natural appearance and not shave saying: 'Let living in His presence, With mind rid of impurities, Be your disciple. Keep the God-given form intact, With a turban donned on your head'. (AG 1084).

It was Guru Gobind Singh who placed an obligation on Sikhs to wear the five articles of faith called the *Panj Kakke* or 5 Ks when he established the Khalsa at Anandpur in 1699.

The Panj Kakke (the five Ks)

1   *Kesh* means hair. The hair is a symbol of faith and keeping long hair confirms a Sikh's belief in the acceptance of God's Will. It emphasises humility and acceptance.
2   *Kangha* means comb. A small wooden comb is worn in the hair. Through the action of the comb in cleaning the hair, Sikhs are reminded how meditation on God's Name removes impurity from the mind. It also symbolises discipline.
3   *Karra* means a link or bondage. A steel bracelet is worn on the right wrist signifying the permanent link or bond with the Gurus and members of the Khalsa. The circle symbolises restraint in behaviour and the unity of God.
4   *Kachha* is a pair of shorts worn under a Sikh's ordinary clothing. They were introduced as an alternative garment to the Hindu dhoti and emphasise spiritual independence.
5   *Kirpan* is a sword symbolising authority, justice and the importance of defending spiritual freedom. Many Sikhs do not carry the kirpan in public and in order to fulfil the obligation replace it with a small kirpan-shaped blade embedded in the kangha.

Sikh women tend to wear trousers (*shalwar*) and a tunic (*kameez*) though those who have been initiated into the Khalsa are also expected to wear the 5 Ks. The *sari* is also popular but this should be worn with the midriff not exposed. Around their shoulders or over their heads women will wear a scarf (*dupatta* or *chunni*) which will be pulled respectfully over the head in the presence of men or within the Gurdwara. *Purdah*, the social separation of men and women, is not permitted in Sikhism though there are, by tradition, occasions when men and women may be separate.

Rites of Passage

Birth

It is customary to bring the child into the presence of the Guru Granth Sahib as soon as it is convenient, and the parents will bring gifts to the Gurdwara on this occasion. Devout families request that the baby is given *amrit*, a symbolic nectar made by dissolving sugar crystals in water. A *granthi* (a custodian of the Gurdwara) may be asked to put the tip of a kirpan in the amrit and touch the baby's tongue with it. Prayer is offered throughout this act and the mother will consume the remaining amrit.

The Guru Granth Sahib is then randomly opened and the first word of the left-hand page is read to the parents. They will select a name beginning with the first letter of this word. The selected name is then declared to the congregation and the appropriate appended common name i.e. Kaur (for a girl) or Singh (for a boy). Though these names are associated with the foundation of the Khalsa they are used by all Sikhs and do not imply initiation. The rite concludes with the distribution of Karah Parshad, the ingredients of which would have been provided by the parents.

Initiation

It is through the rite of initiation that a Sikh becomes a full member of the Khalsa brotherhood. Initiates should be familiar with the basic tenets of the faith and be mature enough to fully comprehend the nature of the obligations to which they are committing themselves. Immediately prior to the ceremony they should have bathed and they must be in possession of the Panj Kakke (5 Ks). Any person who accepts the principles of Sikhism may be 'baptised' and the rite itself may be conducted by five baptised male members of the community, representing the original initiates baptised by Guru Gobind Singh (the Panj Pyares), and the Guru Granth Sahib.

The first part of the ceremony consists of an exposition of the principles of faith, readings from the scriptures and the preparation of the symbolic elixir (*amrit*) in an iron bowl on a pedestal. The liquid is transformed on being stirred with a short double-edged sword (*khanda*) whilst the five squat in the position of the warrior, reciting hymns from the Guru Granth Sahib which constitute an admirable precis of the Sikh faith.

Having reflected upon the teaching, the candidates take up a similar position to the five and are given amrit to drink before it is sprinkled five times on their eyes, face and hair, any residual amrit being consumed by the initiates. During this sequence of events each candidate says 'The Khalsa is of God, the Victory is to God' ('*Waheguru ji ka Khalsa, Waheguru ji ki Fateh*').

The ceremony ends with a lecture on the significance of the obligations accepted by the participants, followed by the *Ardas* prayer and the sharing of Karah Parshad.

Marriage

Sikh marriages are arranged though nowadays the couple are involved in the choice and have the right to accept or reject the proposed partner. Caste and status should not be allowed to dominate the choice of partner nor should astrology feature in the selection.

Marriage is viewed as a religious rite symbolising the spiritual union of the couple with each other and with God. Perhaps this is demonstrated by one particular feature of the ceremony itself when the bride's father puts a garland on the Guru Granth Sahib (which must be present at the ceremony) and then places one over the shoulders of his daughter and the groom. He then binds the end of her head-covering to the scarf worn by the groom or hands her the scarf. As the special wedding hymn, the *Lavan*, is sung the groom leads his bride four times around the Guru Granth Sahib.

Death

According to traditional practices Sikhs are cremated though other forms of disposing of the dead are permitted. Since the concept of rebirth is fundamental excessive grief is regarded as contrary to Sikh beliefs. However, in the hope that God's grace will end the cycle, the *Sohila*, a prayer usually spoken at bedtime, is recited at the funeral. Part of the prayer says: 'If He abides with you undisturbed, you will not be reborn'.

Prior to cremation the body is washed, clothed in clean garments and dressed in the five Ks.

Death is seen as an overt demonstration of the futility of being self-centred and worldly-conscious. Many hymns within the Guru Granth Sahib constantly promote this sentiment. As it says in one of the hymns in the Guru Granth Sahib: 'The dawn of a new day is the herald of a sunset, Earth is not your permanent home'. (AG 793)

SIKHISM

For further reading:

Cole, W. O.	THE GURU IN SIKHISM	Darton, Longman & Todd
Cole, W. O. Sambhi, P.S.	THE SIKHS	R.K.P.
Fraser, G. S.	THE SACRED WRITINGS OF THE SIKHS	Allen & Unwin
James, A. R.	SIKH CHILDREN IN BRITAIN	O.U.P.
Singh, K.	THE SIKHS	Lustre Press Pvt.
Singh, T.	SIKHISM, ITS IDEALS & INSTITUTIONS	Orient Longmans, Calcutta

Short sections on two other world religions

THE BÁHÁ'I FAITH
AND
RASTAFARIANISM

A BASIC INTRODUCTION TO THE BÁHÁ'I FAITH

It is a basic Bahá'í belief that religious truth is not absolute but relative, and that divine revelation is a continuous and progressive process. Consequently all the great religions of the world are divine in origin. Their basic principles are in complete harmony, their aims and purposes are one and the same and they differ only in the non-essential aspects of their doctrines. Their missions represent successive stages in the spiritual evolution of human society.

God reveals His purpose to humanity through a succession of chosen Messengers throughout the ages, according to the needs and capacity of the age. The Bahá'í Faith upholds the unity of God, and the unity of His prophets, inculcates the principle of the oneness of the entire human race and proclaims the necessity and inevitability of the unification of mankind.

In May 1844 in the town of Shiraz in southern Iran, a young man, Siyyid Mirza Ali Muhammad, later known as the Báb ('*Gate*' in Arabic), advanced the claim of being the Herald, who according to past scriptures, would announce and prepare the way for the advent of one greater than himself. The mission of the *Promised One* would be to inaugurate an era of world peace, consummate all previous dispensations and initiate a new cycle in the world's religious history.

Swift and severe persecution launched by the religious leaders and the State resulted in the imprisonment of the Báb, and in July 1850 He was executed in Tabriz. Twenty thousand of His followers were put to death in a wave of persecution.

Mirza Husayn Ali, surnamed Bahá'u'lláh, whose advent the Báb had foretold, was, as a result of the fanatical attacks on the Bábí community, banished, first to Baghdad and thence to Constantinople (Istanbul), Adrianople (Edirne) and finally to Akka in the Holy Land. Here He was imprisoned and He died in 1892, still in exile from His native land.

The Laws and Ordinances of Bahá'u'lláh were formulated in over one hundred volumes and proclaimed in His messages to kings, rulers and ecclesiastics throughout the world.

His eldest son, 'Abdu'l-Bahá, was appointed by Him as the authorised interpreter of His teachings. In 1908, after sixty-four years of exile and imprisonment, He was released from the penal colony of Akka as a consequence of the 'Young Turks' revolution, and embarked on a three year journey to Egypt, Europe and North America. As a result of these journeys, Bahá'í communities grew in the West. In 1920, one year before His passing, Abdu'l-Bahá was knighted by the British Government for His services to humanity.

Abdu'l-Bahá appointed His grandson, Shoghi Effendi, to be the Guardian of the Bahá'í Faith, and under his guidance the Faith spread throughout the world. Shoghi Effendi died during a visit to London in 1957 and is buried in New Southgate Cemetery. Since his passing no single person has had authority over the Bahá'í community as in 1963 the first Universal House of Justice, the supreme ruling body of the Baha'i world, ordained by Bahá'u'lláh, was elected. Elections for this body are held every five years and it consists of nine members who reside in Haifa, the world centre of the Bahá'í Faith.

The Bahá'í Faith is a recognised independent world religion with its own Founder, Holy Days, calendar, scripture and houses of worship. It has no clergy and is administered by local and national spiritual assemblies elected annually and consisting of nine persons.

Its basic principles are the oneness of God, the oneness of religions, the oneness of mankind, the independent investigation of truth, the abolition of all forms of prejudice, compulsory universal education, equal status for men and women, harmony of science and religion, and the need for lasting world peace founded on justice.

The spiritual teachings of the Bahá'í Faith re-state those of previous dispensations (the teachings of Krishna, Zoroaster, Moses, Buddha, Christ and Muhammad): love for one's fellow men; the avoidance of gossip and idle talk; looking for the good in others and bringing one's self to account; truthfulness and reliability; the sanctity of marriage and the necessity of prayer and meditation. Bahá'u'lláh also forbid the use of alcohol and addictive drugs.

The purpose of the Bahá'í revelation is, in the words of its Founder, to *'safeguard the interests and promote the unity of the human race and foster a spirit of love and fellowship amongst men'.*

A BASIC INTRODUCTION TO RASTAFARIANISM

ORIGINS

To many Rastafarians the main inspirer, or prophet, of the Rastafarian Movement was Marcus Garvey. In 1914 he formed the United Negro Improvement Association. Its purpose was to evoke the pride of Black people in their African roots and heritage.

Marcus Garvey suggested that Black people should look towards Africa as their true home and that they should try their best to return. He also predicted the coming of a Black Messiah. Then in Ethiopia, in 1930 Ras Tafari (which translated means Head Creator) was crowned in Addis Ababa as Emperor of Ethiopia and as head of the Ethiopian Orthodox Church. The Church bestowed upon him the name Haile Selassie I (which means power of the holy trinity).

Followers of Marcus Garvey believed Haile Selassie was the Black Messiah whom Garvey had predicted. They believed that Haile Selassie's coming to power was prophesised in the Bible, especially in the book of Revelation. Some of Selassie's titles are 'King of Kings', 'Lord of Lords' and 'Lion of Judah' – titles which are found in the book of Revelation too.

Marcus Garvey's followers now saw Haile Selassie I not just as Emperor but as the Messiah Marcus Garvey had talked about and Marcus Garvey as the John the Baptist who had prepared the way. They came to look on Ethiopia as their true home. (Historically the name 'Ethiopia' was not just restricted to the geographical region known by that name today, but covered the length and breadth of Africa.) They adopted the beliefs and style of worship of the Ethiopian Orthodox Church (one of the oldest Coptic Christian Churches). This was the beginning of what is known as the Rastafarian faith.

BELIEFS & PRACTICES

Appearance

Most Rastafarians grow their hair long, in dreadlocks. This act of growing dreadlocks, involves a vow between the individual and God, that the individual will adhere to a certain way of life. Rastafarians view the flag of Ethiopia with high esteem. The colours of the flag are red, gold and green.

Rastafarians often wear these colours with black. Rastas think these colours symbolise:

Red   – The blood of the Martyrs, Warriors and Slaves that has been shed.

Gold   – The Sun of God, light of this world and Earth's Source of Energy.

Green – The fruitfulness of the earth and Africa's greenery.

Black – The peoples of Africa.

Africa and Babylon

Africa is home to a Rastafarian. Some want to return there. Others see Africa as the symbol of their pride and what they want to achieve – equal rights, justice etc.

At present black people live in many parts of the world. Rastas think of Jamaica or Britain as '*Babylon*' – a place of exile and slavery for them. They see themselves as being like the Israelites who were enslaved in Babylon (Psalm 137 '*The Rivers of Babylon*'). In fact 'Babylon' means, to a Rasta, anything that is viewed as bad – bad people, societies, countries or treatment. The biblical city of Babylon was known for its wickedness, corruption and immoral acts against God. The above word has been incorporated in the Rastafarian vocabulary to mean bad or wicked.

The Bible

The Bible is revered by Rastafarians, particularly *The Kebra Negast* (The Book of Kings), the Holy book of the Ethiopian Orthodox Church, which has the Ethiopian version of the Story of Solomon and Sheba. Sheba was the Ethiopian Queen who visited Solomon in Jerusalem and bore him a son who later reigned in Ethiopia. His name was Menelik I.

Rastas study the Bible. They believe that the Bible prophesies the end of the world, the return of the Messiah and the saving of a chosen few – the Rasta – who believe correctly. They get these beliefs from 'Revelation', and books of prophecy in the Old Testament, like Daniel and Isaiah.

God

The Rastafarians' name for God is '*Jah*', one of the oldest names that God is known by. The name Jah can be found in Psalm 68 v.4.

Rastafarians believe God is inside each person and is a real part of everyone, which is why when talking about themselves they say, '*I and I*'. Also, because they think God is within us, Rastafarians view the human body as the temple of God which must be kept holy.

Rastafarians believe that God is the God of every one so anyone can become a believer. A quotation from a famous Rastafarian, Bob Marley: '*Me don't dip on the black man's side, nor the white man's side, me dip on God's side, the man who created me to come from Black and White*' (Marley's father was a white Englishman)'.

Ten Commandments

A true Rastafarian lives his or her life in accordance to the ten commandments of Moses, all other disciplines evolve around this belief.

Food

Rastas follow the food laws laid down in the Old Testament. They are forbidden to eat pork, because this is regarded as unclean, nor will they touch alcohol because this is believed to be an instrument of enslavement. Orthodox Rastafarians are non-drinkers and strict vegetarians. They try to eat only naturally grown food – 'I-Tal' food.

Music

A lot of reggae music is inspired by Rastafarianism. Many reggae bands in Britain in fact preach their religion when they sing.

Women

Rastafarians disapprove of all Church marriages outside the Ethiopian Orthodox Church. Rastafarian women are treated with respect, they are expected to keep their hair covered, the straightening of the hair and cosmetic make-up are frowned upon.

It is generally accepted that the man is the head of the family, and that the woman is the head of the household. Rastafarian women are expected to treat all men with respect. They are also expected to walk and talk in a dignified manner. The use of swear words by women is frowned upon. In the Rastafarian faith the women are known as queens and the men as kings.

Ganja (herb)

Most Rastafarians view *ganja* as a holy plant. They believe that cannabis smoking is suggested in the Bible as a way of purifying the smoker and of helping thought, or meditation on the truth. Rastas regard Ganja as a holy sacrament – that is something to be used in religious ceremonies for symbolic reasons.

GENERAL INTRODUCTIONS TO WORLD RELIGIONS

Bowker, J. (ed.)	THE OXFORD COMPANION TO RELIGIONS OF THE WORLD	O.U.P.
Crimm, K. (ed.)	THE ABINGDON DICTIONARY OF LIVING RELIGIONS	Abingdon Nashville
Hinnells, J. (ed.)	A HANDBOOK OF LIVING RELIGIONS	Viking
Hinnells, J. (ed.)	THE PENGUIN DICTIONARY OF RELIGIONS	
Smart, N.	THE RELIGIOUS EXPERIENCE OF MANKIND	Fontana
Zachner, R. C. (ed.)	THE CONCISE ENCYCLOPEDIA OF LIVING RELIGIONS	Hutchinson

ACKNOWLEDGMENTS

The authors wish to record their thanks to the following contributors and consultants who helped with the production of this booklet:

Mr John Bailey	Chief Inspector
Dr Owen Cole	West Sussex Institute of Higher Education
Mr Ken Oldfield	West London Institute of Higher Education
Dr Madhufudan Gandhi	President, Shree Sanatan Seva Samaj
Mr Cyril Davis	President, Luton Synagogue
Mr Michael Shaw	Maidenhall Junior School
Mrs Pauline Poulton	Manjushri Buddhist Sanga
The Revd Terry Beaumont	Vicar, St. Peter's Church, Broadwater, Stevenage
The Revd Fr. Sean Healy	Chairman, Luton Council of Churches
Imam Mohammed Ikram Choudry	Member of Luton Muslim Community
Mrs Misbah Parvaz	Farley Junior School
Mr Syed Rizvi	Central Mosque, Luton
Mr Jaswinder Singh Nagra	President, International Sikh Youth Federation
Mr Amar Sanghera	Drake Lower School
Mr Michael Gammage	Assembly of the Baha'is of Luton
Mr Derrick Spalding	Member of Luton Rastafarian Community

Working papers from the 'World Religions in Luton' series of meetings (Summer 1984) have also been used as a source of information.